Teach Your Child About Money Through Play

110+ Games/Activities, Tips and Resources to Teach Kids Financial Literacy at an Early Age

---

BY

ANDREA STEPHENSON WITH LINSEY MILLS

Copyright © 2019 by Andrea Stephenson and Linsey Mills

All rights reserved. This book or any portion thereof may not be reproduced or used in any manner whatsoever without the express written permission of the publisher.

www.SimplyOutrageousYouth.org | Amills@SimplyOutrageousYouth.org

| Callinz.com | LinseyMills.com

DEDICATION

To my mother, Patricia Mills.

You are my biggest supporter. I can count on you to be the first to read my work and provide feedback. Thank you for encouraging me to keep a journal of my activities. I was afraid to put my work out in the world, but you inspired me to push past my fear. I appreciate all the early lessons in financial literacy you gave me. Because of you, I was not afraid to handle money and knew what it meant to have a good credit score. Keep being you and thank you for everything.

I love you,

Andrea

To my parents, Calvin Ray Mills and Patricia Jean Mills,

You were the first financial advisors from whom I learned the fundamentals of financial literacy. There were many disciplines that you practiced as a way of life that helped me learn the value of money. I also learned from your challenges as a working-class family in Jacksonville, North Carolina. There were many, but they proved to be a good starting point for me as I began working at the age of sixteen and earning my own money. As I enter my twenty-seventh year in the financial services business, my goal is to continue sharing innovative and engaging financial literacy lessons and experiences with young people.

Linsey

REVIEWS

This book is a fantastic resource for parents and educators alike who want to teach kids real money skills in a way they can understand and enjoy. The activities are unique, fun, and engaging and can be tailored to writers and pre-writers alike.

—Stacey K., Editor, Birmingham, Alabama

I wish I knew then what I know now…' I've said this hundreds of times throughout my thirty's. That is why I am so enthralled with Teach Your Child about Money Through Play by Andrea Stephenson and Linsey Mills.

I love that this book gives children an understanding of money and finances. Not only does it delve into ideas that make money, but it teaches the facts of money; its purpose, how to use money as a tool to grow in all areas of our lives and other vehicles that help accumulate financial growth.

However, the true genius of this book is two-fold; first, it is full of practical applications which drive home the relevance and importance of each lesson; liabilities and assets, good and bad debt management, creating investment portfolios and starting your own entrepreneurial business endeavor, to name a few. Real information that can net you real results.

Teach Your Child about Money Through Play simplifies what can be a daunting topic. It is a wonderful tool for a family to go through together. Perhaps you have a strong understanding of financial literacy; it will help you with ways to easily teach that information to your children or sphere of influence. If you don't have quite a firm hold on financial literacy, it will let you and your child bond over the information and complete the activities together so the whole family grows.

Andrea Stephenson and Linsey Mills have put together an incredible guide to financial literacy for children (and adults), but the real winners are the readers. You are embarking on an incredible journey, and the authors have prepared the perfect itinerary.

Elliott Eddie, https://entrepreneurboardgame.com

ABOUT ME

Hello, and thank you for taking the time to learn more about teaching financial literacy to kids. My name is Linsey Mills. I'm Andrea's older brother, and it's exciting to be part of this book and share with you the concepts we learned while growing up in a rural working-class family located in Jacksonville, North Carolina. Afterward, we both furthered our formal education at Davidson College located in Davidson, North Carolina.

I am a financial consultant and educator with over twenty years' experience in the financial services industry. Over those years, I have looked for opportunities to create programs, tools and activities that create an environment where children can be inspired and have fun learning opportunities about money and finances. One of the most successful of those programs is called TRADER$: Stock Market Experience.

I learned the fundamental concepts of saving, return on investment, and doing financial transactions from my parents. They had me making deposits at the bank, writing checks, and counting money. Andrea shares many of those activities with you in this book. As a college student and adult, I developed some of my own activities, role plays and concepts that were helpful to Andrea, and hopefully to you as you continue reading.

ANDREA STEPHENSON

www.SimplyOutrageousYouth.org

AMills@SimplyOutrageousYouth.com

Follow Simply Outrageous Youth on:

Pinterest

Facebook

Instagram

YouTube

LINSEY MILLS

CallinzGroup.com

Callinz.com

LinseyMills.com

Follow me on:

@LinseyMills on Twitter

Contents

Chapter 1: The Purpose 1

Chapter 2: Introducing Young Kids to Money 12

Chapter 3: Money – What's the Use? 29

Chapter 4: How Do People Get Money? 42

Chapter 5: Budgeting 64

Chapter 6: Basic Banking 76

Chapter 7: Liabilities and Assets 88

Chapter 8: Good Debt, Bad Debt 101

Chapter 9: Real Estate 117

Chapter 10: Stocks, Bonds, and Mutual Funds 135

Chapter 11: Starting a Business 149

Chapter 12: Field Trips and Real-World Activities 180

Chapter 13: Bonus Chapter: Insurance 197

Favorite Resources 207

CHAPTER 1

The Purpose

WHY THIS BOOK WAS WRITTEN

Financial Literacy and Our Public-School System

Financial literacy is a subject that we all can agree is important to learn. Unfortunately, it is a subject that is not taught in many public schools. I have always wondered why this is the case. The American public school system became popular in the 1850s. By 1900, thirty-one states required children to attend public schools from the ages of eight to fourteen. As this concept became popular in 1918, all states required children to complete at least elementary school. In the 1920s, schools focused on math, English, and social studies.

Today 93 percent of children attend public school while being exposed to the following subjects: English, math, science, social studies, language arts, and more. However, you will rarely hear that children are being exposed to financial literacy in schools.

In my research, I have found that our modern education system was designed to teach up-and-coming factory workers to be punctual and obedient. Factory owners wanted great workers who did their jobs and adhered to their manager's rules. If you think about it, sitting in a classroom for most of the day with a teacher is the ideal training for this future.

So maybe financial literacy is missing from schools to keep us coming back to work daily. This means going to work, getting paid, spending money on expenses such as our mortgage/rent, food, gas, and clothing, and then repeating the cycle. This cycle is repeated because we need more money to pay for food, clothes, and mortgage/rent each month.

Whatever the reason, we all can agree that teaching children financial literacy is important. When our children become adults, most likely they will have to deal with money. They will need money for basic living necessities such as shelter, water, food, transportation, and clothing. Many adults take it a step further by buying cars, going on vacation, buying digital media equipment, owning a business, and investing money. It takes money to acquire all of these things. If a child has financial literacy skills, then most likely they will make smart decisions.

My Family Was on the Right Track
From Andrea's Point of View

My first lesson in financial literacy was from my parents and my older brother, Linsey. Linsey is eleven years older than me. He taught me how to recognize money and its value. I remember sitting in our den reviewing the monetary value of the coins and dollar bills with Linsey. The practice of touching money, comparing its sizes, and learning who was on the coins and dollars was simple yet so effective. It was also a great opportunity for me to bond with Linsey.

After I understood the monetary value of money, my mom created opportunities for me to count money. My mother saved all her coins in a big jar within our home. When the first week of December came, she instructed me to sort the pennies, nickels, dimes, and quarters. She would give me the pennies to put in wrappers. This simple activity taught me so much. I learned how to sort money into categories, count fifty pennies at a time, and position them in the coin wrapper so they would not fall out. I quickly learned that by counting the pennies by tens, I would get to fifty quicker.

I also learned that pennies really add up to make dollars! From that experience, I rarely bypass an unclaimed penny in the couch or on the floor. All you have to do is wash it, and the value of the penny comes alive. My four-year-son has learned the same values. Whenever he sees coins that no one is claiming, he will ask if he can have them.

My dad taught me about the movement and exchange of money. I grew up in a time where most people used cash to pay for small items such as food, gas, and clothes. As a child, I would accompany him on errands to grocery stores, to pay bills, etc. Whenever he bought something, he allowed me to give the cashier the money to purchase the item. He made me conscious of how much the item cost and the amount of money I got back in change. Before I was able to subtract my change back from a cashier, I knew to stand there and get money back unless he told me I didn't need it. After I learned to subtract, I would always check to ensure the cashier gave me back the correct amount.

Paying Bills

One of the biggest lessons we learn as adults is paying bills. Some people are nervous about doing this because it can impact their credit score, borrowing power, and future purchases. There are others who go with the flow and learn about the process of paying bills as life happens.

My mother prepared me well to pay bills. After I was able to write in cursive, she would have me sit at the table to complete checks and money orders, which is a printed payment of a specified amount issued by a bank or post office, to pay the utility bills. After my task was done, she would sign the checks or money orders. Sometimes I would complete the money orders and checks in the car. She'd ask me to pull out the water bill and write out a check for that amount.

Furthermore, I would go into the convenience store with her to get the money orders. I learned that money orders came with a small fee, but could be replaced if lost. Once I got my driver's license, she would give me copies of some of the bills, and it was my job to pay them with the money orders and checks she provided.

While in graduate school, I lived alone in a St. Louis, Missouri, apartment. During this time, I was responsible for my rent, gas, water, electricity, and graduate school bill. I was excited to take on this responsibility because it gave me the opportunity to put my financial literacy lessons learned during childhood into practice. My determination to pay all my bills early or on time was very strong.

It was during these times I started to read books on financial literacy and business. I quickly learned that the way to pay for my living expenses and extra items I wanted was to create an asset.

Financial Literacy Education Continued

During my middle and high school years, Linsey and my sister-in-law, Michelle, invited me stay with them for two to three weeks in the summers. They owned two businesses, and my job was to work and learn. Our Story Consulting was the first business, and this was a consulting and desktop publishing company. The second business was called PositiviTees, a custom-design T-shirt company which featured golf lines of clothing U Da Man and U Golf Girl. In 1997, Linsey was recognized as the Small Business Administration Young Entrepreneur of the Year for the Southeast Region of the United States.

Linsey and Michelle taught me about the stock market, credit cards, interest, customer service in business, profit, loss, etc. I learned all of this through experience in working in their businesses, playing financial literacy games, and role plays they created. I remember one time, they dressed up in different characters pretending to buy a home, and I had to calculate the amount of interest they would pay. Their stock market game, called TRADER$: Stock Market Experience, was crucial in teaching me how the stock market works.

Changing My Perspective About Money

One summer, when I was seventeen, my brother gave me the book *Rich Dad Poor Dad*, by Robert Kiyosaki. This book changed my mentality about money. It was one of the first times I learned simple definitions for the financial terms *liabilities* and *assets*. Kiyosaki said *assets* are things that put money in your pocket and *liabilities* are things that take money out of your pocket. These were concepts young children could learn with ease.

I also learned the various lessons that rich and poor people teach their kids. The difference between an employee, self-employed person, business owner, and investor were clear to me after reading this book. Then my brother and sister-in-law took my learning further through playing board games.

Cashflow and Monopoly

One day my brother and I were in his office and he pulled out the game Cashflow 101. It was a bright purple and yellow board game with an enormous rat on the front. Once my brother opened the box, I saw pencils, games pieces, a game board, and financial sheets that looked intimidating. Initially, I was a little nervous to play this game. However, once we started playing, I started to understand how to complete the financial sheet and learned how the rich think about money. It was a definite eye-opener.

I then learned that the creator of Cashflow 101 created a game for children called Cashflow for Kids. I purchased this game in my twenties because I wanted to introduce this concept to children I was teaching in after-school programs. They loved this game, by the way!

Afterward, I thought maybe I would try to introduce the concept of real estate to the children in the after-school program. In the Robert Kiyosaki books, he talks about Monopoly being a wonderful game to introduce kids to real estate. The next week, I played Monopoly with the kids but added the concept of assets and liabilities within the game. Again, they learned so much and enjoyed themselves.

My experiences and study taught me that kids can learn financial literacy, and the best way to do it is through games and real-world experiences.

Introducing Kids to Financial Literacy in a Fun Manner

While in graduate school, I started the Simply Outrageous Youth (SOY) brand. Linsey created the Simply Outrageous brand, which is a marketing company that developed innovative programs like Simply Outrageous Math and trained individuals to become entrepreneurs through Linsey's first book, *Simply Outrageous: Lessons Learned on the Road to Entrepreneur of the Year*.

I had a contract with local after-school and summer programs in the St. Louis area to teach kids in the third through eighth grades financial literacy. The Masters of Business Administration (MBA) students volunteered to teach (and add on to, of course) the financial literacy curricula I created, to the students. We taught the kids through interactive games and activities.

After graduate school, I worked for a small business named Entrenuity in Chicago owned by Brian Jenkins. I worked in communities such as Cabrini Green teaching children how to start their own businesses. We helped hundreds of children start businesses. One group of kids created Chi-Town Jewelry and made over $1,000 in revenue within a year.

Working at Entrenuity also allowed me to start a Business Summer Camp at Wheaton College. I was the camp director and helped the owner, Brian Jenkins, create the curricula for the camp.

After two years of working at Entrenuity, my next step was to grow the Simply Outrageous Youth brand. I wanted to use the same educational business formula from graduate school, but in the city and suburbs of Philadelphia, Pennsylvania. This time I hired twenty-five teachers to go into the after-school and summer programs to teach my curricula. By this time, the curricula expanded beyond financial literacy to conflict resolution, leadership, social skills, and more.

During this time, I met a wonderful man named Lyndon, who is now my husband. Four years after getting married, we had a son, Cory. Once my son was born, I knew that I would expose him to financial literacy in a fun way. My original thoughts were to teach him once he turned five or six. However, with my son's curiosity and fast learning pace, I started when he was fifteen months. I will show you how in the next chapter.

TIP #1

Use real-world experiences to expose kids to financial literacy.

TIP #2

Use interactive games to expose kids to financial literacy.

TIP #3

Have your children participate with you in your encounters of exchanging money.

CHAPTER 2

Introducing Young Kids to Money

HOW WE STARTED

Robert Kiyosaki, the author of *Rich Dad Poor Dad*, said that when you are an adult, your report card is your credit score. This is one reason why teaching kids financial literacy is so important. Once a child becomes an adult, handling money becomes inevitable. So I am striving to build an early foundation in my child!

The Beginning

My son, like many children, has always been curious about the world around him. The first time he saw a coin, it was on a table. He held it up, and I told him it was a quarter that is worth twenty-five cents. Cory looked at it for a while, tossed it in the air, and was amazed when he heard the loud sound it made when it hit the floor. I observed how interested he was in this shiny coin and decided maybe it was time to show him a piggy bank.

We received two piggy banks at our baby shower. We put them in Cory's room so he could see them daily. I brought one of the piggy banks downstairs along with a bag full of coins I saved and showed them to Cory. I could see his eyes getting big with amazement at the sight of all those coins.

My purpose was to let him touch, feel, and play with coins. Cory was fifteen months at this time, so I stayed close to him. I did not want him to put the money in his mouth. He carefully took pennies, nickels, dimes, and quarters out of the plastic bag and put them in the piggy bank. He was pleased with the clanging sound made as the coins hit the bottom of the piggy bank.

The act of handling and transferring the coins was his first hands-on lesson in money. It got him interested in wanting to learn more about money's purpose and value. It also prepared him for his next task with money, which was sorting it by shape and size and learning its monetary value.

Cory putting money in piggy bank as a one-year-old

Continuing to Explore Coins

Cory practiced putting coins in the piggy bank several times before he sorted them. I also wanted to make further real-world connections with money, so I got him children's books on the subject. One of the most engaging books we read was *Money Math Addition and Subtraction* by David A. Adler and Edward Miller.

We also identified coins when we saw them on the table, couch, and outside. He became especially good at spotting coins on the ground and in other family members' homes. If it was a close family member like my mom, then I would let him ask her if he could keep it. Otherwise, I would encourage him to observe the coin and leave it be.

Sorting

Cory became an expert at sorting coins after his third Christmas. My mom continued to save coins in a jar all year, but this time instead of spending all the money on Christmas gifts, she gave a majority of the coins to my son. Now that she had a grandson, she would give the coins to Cory to fund his Christmas gifts or to save. I took some of the money to buy him a gift, and the other part I put in a bank account for my son.

In order to prepare for this moment, I purchased the Nadex Sort and Wrap Set from Amazon three months before Christmas. This set comes with four coin-sorting trays, four easy-wrap coin tubes, and 352 coin wrappers. There are 88 color-coded wrappers for the quarters, nickels, dimes, and pennies. Cory and I saved coins throughout the year, and he used them to purchase Christmas gifts for family members.

This activity provided a great opportunity for Cory to learn the size difference and monetary value of money. It was also a time to learn patience and to practice counting. This would be a time-consuming task that would take more than one session. Furthermore, he was learning the lesson of giving instead of receiving all the time.

Back when I was a child putting coins in the wrappers, I had to hold the bottom of the wrapper with one hand and insert pennies with the other. The Nadex Sort and Wrap Set saves time and makes things easier. Cory simply inserted the wrapper and coins in the tube, and it has a line that tells the user when the right number of coins has been inserted. Then you slide the wrapper out of the tube, and your coins are wrapped quickly.

Many times, instead of using the line in the tube, Cory and I counted the coins to practice some math skills. We repeated this activity at least three times before going to my mom's home.

The Big Day

We were at my mom's house during the Christmas holiday, and then we saw a huge jar of coins. My mom told Cory it was his job to sort the coins and put them in the appropriate wrapper. I sent her pictures, three months beforehand, of Cory putting the coins and wrappers in the Nadex Sort and Wrap Set. She saw how engaged and interested he was in the activity. Linsey sat down with my son and they started putting the coins in wrappers using the Nadex Sort and Wrap Set. It seemed like they had a good time and got a lot of wrapping done.

We took the rest of the coins home and finished wrapping them there. Then we took the coins to the bank and deposited the money.

My son putting coins in the wrappers.

Linsey's Point of View on Wrapping Coins with Cory

I loved counting money as a child. Every week I emptied my piggy bank (bank safe with combination) to count my money. It was fun to engage in this activity with Cory. Counting coins engages all of the senses and math skills. This tradition of saving coins was passed down from our dad, who always saved jars of coins at home and at work. Before I started working for money, my parents allowed me to keep their coin change from purchases when I did the transaction.

ACTIVITIES

Becoming Familiar with Money

The **value of money** and how to count it is a basic skill every child should learn. The activities below teach money recognition in a fun way.

- The first step in money recognition is for kids to hold and interact with money.
- Give your child a bunch of coins in a bowl or bag.
- Have your child put money in a piggy bank.
- Stay close to your child if they are very young.
- Optional: Start introducing them to the money value by identifying each coin and its value as they put it in the piggy bank.
- Don't quiz them on this information right now. You are identifying the coins and their value as an introduction at this point.

Sort Money

- Put coins you have collected in a pile.
- Help your child sort the coins by pennies, nickels, dimes, quarters, half dollars, etc.

- Help your child learn the difference in colors and sizes. Identify the following:
    - Pennies are a brownish copper color.
    - Dimes are the smallest coins.
    - Quarters are the biggest coins.
    - If you have half dollars available, then they are the biggest.
    - Nickels are bigger than dimes and pennies but smaller than quarters.
- Optional: start introducing your child to the money value by identifying each coin and its value as they put it in the piggy bank.

Make a Trip to the Bank

Materials needed:

- Coins
- Money jar or bag
- Coin wrappers (your local bank or credit union may be able to provide this)
- Optional: Nadex Sort and Wrap Set

Directions:

- Have the child gather loose coins and put into money jar.
- Count the coins and sort into money wrappers using the Nadex Sort and Wrap Set (optional).

- You may also put coins in the wrapper the old-fashion way without the Nadex Sort and Wrap Set.
- Take the coins to the bank or credit union and exchange for cash.
  - If you don't have enough coins to fill wrappers, then check with your local bank about the loose coin conversion policy.
- Deposit the money into a bank account for your child.

Monetary Value of Each Coin

Expose your child to the monetary value of each coin by doing the following:

- Have your child repeat the Sort Money Activity above by having the child sort coins.
- Make colorful signs with the value of money.
- Create a sign for each coin and place it near each type of coin.
- The signs should read the following:
  - Pennies = 1¢
  - Nickels = 5¢
  - Dimes = 10¢
  - Quarters = 25¢
  - Half dollars = 50¢
- Review the values frequently.

- Optional: If you don't want to make colorful signs, then get an automated toy bank. These banks count the money as the kids are dropping the coins or inputting dollars.

Reinforce the Monetary Value of Each Coin with Digital Media

The activities below will help your child learn and reinforce the value of money in an engaging manner.

- Watch the value of money videos on YouTube
  - "The Money Song" by Jack Hartmann
  - "Counting Coins Song for Kids" by Math Songs by Numerock
  - "Learn to Name and Count US Coins" by Rock N' Learn
  - "Money Song" by Mark D. Pencil and Friends
  - "Learning Money for Kids/Coin Song for Children/Money Song for Kid" by Kids Learning Tube
  - "Coin Song.WMV" by Holly Raser
  - "Coins!" by ABCmouse.com

Give Me the Money!

Cory and I play this game with his toy cash register. It teaches kids money recognition.

Materials needed:

- Stuffed animal or toy action figure
- Toy cash register or play money
- You may also make your own play money with paper and markers

Directions:

- Give your child the cash register with money or play money.
- Take the stuffed animal or toy action figure and do the next steps.
- Tell your child their stuffed animal or toy action figure is hungry.
- The only thing the toy will eat is money.
- Ask your child to give you various coins.
    - For example, ask your child to give you one penny.
- If they give you the correct coin, then pretend like the toy is eating the coin.
- If your child gives you the wrong coin, then have the toy say, "Ewww, yucky!"
- Continue to ask your child to give you various coins.
- Then ask your child to give you various dollars.
- If your child gets good at this game, make it more difficult by doing the following:

- Ask them to give you two or three coins instead of one.
- Ask them to give you a certain amount of money, like 26¢ or $1.28.

- Make this game even more fun by switching roles, where your child asks you to give them a certain amount of money (once they understand the concept).

Money Hunt Activity

Materials needed:

- Play money
- You may use real money if you like, but I would not advise it.

Directions:

- Hide coins and dollars in one room of your house.
- Tell your child to find the money in that room.
- You may tell them the amount of money you hid, such as four quarters, two dimes, and three nickels.
- Have your child find the money around the room.
- Once they have found all the money, have them identify what money they found and the value associated with it.
  - For instance, if they found one dollar and two quarters, they should communicate this to you.

- If your child gets good at this game, make it more difficult by doing the following:
  - Have the child add the total amount they found.

Behind the Back

My son made up this game. This game will help children practice their money recognition skills.

Materials needed:

- Play money or toy cash register with money
- If you don't have play money, make your own with paper and art supplies.

Directions:

- Tell your child to close their eyes.
- Get one piece of money from the cash register while your child's eyes are closed and put it behind your back.
  - It could be one dollar, five dollars, ten dollars, or a twenty-dollar bill.
  - You can also get coins, such as a penny, nickel, dime, quarter, or half dollar.
- Give your child clues about the money you have behind your back.

- If you have a five-dollar bill behind your back, then the following could be your clue:
  - This bill has Abraham Lincoln on it.
  - It has the number 5 on it.
- Now your child must guess what is behind your back.
- Now switch roles
- You close your eyes.
- Have your child pick one piece of money from the cash register and put it behind their back.
- Your child will give you clues as to what is hiding behind their back.
- You have to guess what it is based off their clues.

Read Children's Books About Money

- Read books about the value of money.
- Along with reading, have real or play money beside you.
- While you are reading about a certain coin or dollar, have the child hold that particular money in their hand.
  - For example, if you are reading about a penny, have the child pick one up and hold it.
  - After reading about the penny, talk about the color, writing on the coin, and president Abraham Lincoln's image on it.
- Read books about the value of money such as the following:

- *Money Math* by David Adler
- *The Penny Pot: Counting Coins* by Stuart J. Murphy/Lynne Woodcock Cravath
- *Dollars and Sense* by Stan and Jan Berenstain
- *The Piggybank Blessing* by Stan and Jan Berenstain
- *Bunny Money* by Rosemary Wells

Cory sorting money.

Cory using a money funnel to sort money.

Cory inserting a new wrapper in the money funnel.

CHAPTER 3

Money – What's the Use?

WHERE DID MONEY COME FROM?

Brief History of Money

Since the beginning of time, humans have needed basic items such as food and clothing. They acquired these things by bartering, which is a way of trading. Bartering means exchanging objects you have for something you want. For instance, a family may give green beans to their neighbor, who has chickens, in return for meat.

However, there were problems with the bartering system. What if your neighbor already had green beans? This makes it difficult for the family to get meat. In this case, something was needed that could be used by everyone to exchange for goods. This was a problem that needed to be solved worldwide.

Different cultures and ethnic groups had their own systems of money. The Aztecs used small doll figures made of solid gold and cocoa beans to buy things. Ancient Egyptians and Celts both liked to wear their form of money. Ancient Egyptians used ring money, which is a ring made of bronze copper and gold. The Celts in Ireland used bracelets as well as ring money. In some parts of Africa, cowrie shells, salt, and knife money were used.

In other parts of the world, food items such as rice, bread, or chocolate were used as money. However, these things were difficult to use because sometimes the food would spoil or be eaten before bartering.

In order to solve this problem, money had to be accepted as value by others, have an assigned value, be easily portable, and be durable enough to be handled by a lot of people.

The use of coins was the first solution to this problem. Coins as money first appeared in Turkey, and the idea spread all over the world. The coins had value and were easy to carry around. Each country's coin fit their culture and ethnic personality. For example, the Greeks had gods and goddesses on their coins. The Indians used pictures of dragons on their coins. The Chinese had holes in the center of their coins so they could put them on a string or rope.

Furthermore, the Chinese invented paper, which led to the creation of paper money. Paper money was ideal because it was lightweight, easy to carry, could be decorated, and was predictable.

What Is Money Used for Today?

Money is a banknote. A banknote is a paper by which a bank promises to pay someone who wants various items. It is used as a tool for exchange or trade. When you take your child to the store and buy a stuffed bear, both you and the cashier agree that the banknote used symbolizes a certain value or amount. If the bear costs $5, then you would give the cashier money valuing that amount or more, such as a $5, $10, or $20 bill.

There are four functions of money. It is a medium of exchange, unit of account, store of value, and deferred payment.

Let's discuss *medium of exchange* first. This goes back to the bartering system discussed previously in this chapter. Humans previously acquired basic necessities through bartering. However, this system had problems because it was difficult to find items of equal value to trade. Remember, the family needed chicken but only had green beans to trade with their neighbor. The neighbor already had green beans and could not trade with the family. Paper money and coins solved this problem because they are accepted by everyone in all trades and exchanges.

The second function is as a *unit of account*, which means there is a common value placed on the goods and services exchanged. Let's take our stuffed bear example used previously. The store is selling the stuffed bear for $5, but you as the parent must decide if that is a price you are willing to pay for the bear. If a lot of parents like this bear and are willing to pay $5 for it, then the store will most likely have a lot of bears to make their customers happy.

The third function is as a *store of value*, which means it holds its value over time. This means you can buy the stuffed bear at $5 on Monday and then come back in the next two months and buy the same bear for $5. You may also choose not to buy the bear for $5 and put the money in your child's piggy bank. However, that same $5 bill can be used to buy another toy for $5.

The fourth function is as a *deferred payment*, which is also called *debt*. This means you can buy an item now and pay for it later. Let's say you want to buy a bed for your child at a furniture store and it costs $500. However, you don't have that much money. Then the furniture store will set up a deferred payment plan for you. They may tell you to pay $50 the day you take the bed home, then pay $50 monthly until $500 is paid in full. With this plan, it will take you a total of ten months to pay for the bed in full.

What Can Money Buy?

Money can buy anything that has a price on it. You will see prices on homes, food, clothing, furniture, games, computers, cars, water, etc. It can also buy experiences like when you take your child to an amusement park or zoo. Many times, you have to pay an admission fee to get into these places.

I could go on and on about what money can buy. But let's remember there are things money can't buy. These include love, happiness, talent, true friends, and manners.

There should be a balance between things money can and cannot buy.

In the Activities section, I will show you how to teach your child these concepts through interactive activities and games.

ACTIVITIES

Bartering Game

This game will help your child understand the bartering system used in historical times.

Materials needed:

- List of your child's talents or skills
- Paper
- Writing utensils

Directions:

- Have your child make a list of their skills or talents.
- These skills or talents may include being an excellent cleaner or singer.
- Next, have your child make a list of two wants or needs.
- This may include a toy from an older sibling or a beverage to drink.
- Have your child figure out how they can get one of their wants or needs using their skills or talent.
- For example, if your child wants their older brother's toy, they may clean their brother's room for a day in order to get the toy.

Barter Club

Materials needed:

- At least two children (the more children the better).
- Each child should bring two items of their choice.
- They may also provide a list of skills, services, or talents they can provide for other children.

Directions:

- Have the children gather in one area of your home or even outside.
- Encourage children to barter or trade the items they bought or talents they possess for new items or services.
- Establish before the game begins whether children can keep the items they barter or give them back at the end.

Create Your Own Money

Similar to the Africans, Greeks, and Indians, have your child create their own money.

Materials needed:

- Paper
- Art supplies such as paint, markers, crayons, glue, construction paper, glitter, etc.

Directions:

- Give each child paper.
- Have the art supplies accessible to all students.
- Instruct your child to create their own paper money and coin.
- The following can be included on their paper money and coin.
    - Value or amount of money
    - Picture of something or someone
    - Short message
    - Any type of design your child wants
- Have your child tell you about their money and coin after they complete this task.

Money Buy House Hunt

This activity will give your child an idea of what items in your home cost money.

Materials needed:

- Paper
- Writing utensil

Directions:

- Make a chart with two columns on a piece of paper.
- In one column write the word *Yes*, and in the other put *No*.

- Tell your child you will do a house hunt together.
- You may choose to do this activity within one room or the whole house.
- Find various items in your home such as chairs, tables, toys, food, water, etc.
- Once you find these items, have your child tell you whether they believe money was involved in buying it.
- If the answer is yes, have them write or draw the item in the yes column.
- Then have them tell you how much they believe it costs (optional).
- If the answer is no, have them write or draw the item in the no column.
- Compare the items in both columns and discuss your results.

Money Buy Outside Hunt

This activity is similar to the Money Buy House Hunt Activity, but it is done outside.

Materials needed:

- Notepad or paper
- Writing utensil

Directions:

- Make a chart with two columns on a piece of paper.
- In one column write *Yes*, and in the other put *No*.
- Tell your child you will do an outside hunt together.
- You may choose to do this activity in your backyard, at a park, etc.
- Find various items outside, such as grass, slides, trees, swings, animals, streets, etc.
- Once you find these items, have your child tell you whether they believe money was involved in buying it.
- If the answer is yes, then have them write or draw the item in the yes column.
- Then have them tell you how much they believe it costs (optional).
- If the answer is no, then have them write or draw the item in the no column.
- Compare the items in both columns and discuss your results.

Exchange of Money Ice Cream Store

This activity will teach your child about the exchange of money and its value in a fun way. It also introduces your child to **entrepreneurship**.

Materials needed:

- Play-Doh
- Paper
- Writing utensil
- Play money

Directions:

- Create ice cream by using the following suggestions.
    - Make ice cream with Play-Doh.
    - You may also put various colored balls in cups to make pretend-play ice cream.
    - Another option is to purchase an ice cream set like the Melissa & Doug Scoop & Serve Ice Cream Counter.
- Create price tags and put them on the ice cream.
- Get pretend-play money and give to the customer.
    - We (my son and I) used a toy cash register.
- Have your child play the ice cream store owner.
- As the customer, start by giving your child the correct amount of money for the ice cream.
- Once they become more advanced, give them more than enough money and help them determine the correct change to give you.

- This is also a great activity to teach your child about kindness and customer service.

My son giving me change after my ice cream purchase.

Ice cream cones made from Play-Doh.

CHAPTER 4

How Do People Get Money?

HOW DO PEOPLE EARN MONEY?

Employees

There are many ways people earn money. The first way is through working a job. People who work at a job are called *employees*. An *employee* is a person who is hired by a company to do a certain task. They usually have to complete an application and interview with people who already work for the company. If the company likes the person applying and interviewing, they will hire or give them the job. The company will determine how much the new employee gets paid for doing a job within a certain amount of time.

People who have jobs receive a paycheck or money for the work they perform. The money they receive is called earned income. When money is earned through a paycheck, then that person is trading time for money.

People have jobs to solve problems or to fill a need, and there are many ways to do this. For example, an engineer's job is to use math and science to design and build products, machines, systems, and structures. They want to know how things work, and they make things practical. A plumber is another person that solves problems and fills a need. They are responsible for the system of pipes that brings water to faucets and appliances. Pipes can also remove waste and bring natural gas to the home. We need plumbers to install and maintain the plumbing systems.

Some people have to go to college to work at a certain job, like a medical doctor. Doctors have to go to school between twenty-one and thirty years. Their job is important because they help keep us healthy and make us feel better when we get sick or hurt. They also conduct wellness checks in which they ensure people are functioning in a healthy manner. Then other people, like electricians, have to go to trade school between nine months and six years. Electricians ensure our lighting systems work in our homes and buildings.

Employees can work full time, which is forty hours per week in the United States, or part time, which is less than forty hours per week. Employees usually use money to pay for their basic necessities or needs such as their house or apartment, food, water, electricity, gas, etc. Those who have money left over may buy things they want, such as a car, vacation, or entertainment, like going to the movies.

Business Owners

Another way that people earn money is by owning a business or being an entrepreneur. Business owners are those who have an idea to solve a problem and fulfill a need. They use this idea to start a business, which is an organization where people work together. Business owners usually hire employees to make and sell products or services. Businesses need employees to make more products and serve more people.

For example, a National Basketball Association (NBA) Franchise such as the Los Angeles Lakers is a business. They hire the best basketball players in the world as employees to provide a service to their customers. The service they provide is entertainment. People love to relax and watch competitive basketball games. The people watching the game are called *basketball fans*. Fans cheer for their favorite team hoping they beat the opposing team.

Another type of business is one that sells products like toys. One popular toy company is called Melissa & Doug. They make toys for kids to spark their imagination, help them explore, and encourage creativity. When they make a new toy, they distribute or sell it in stores such as Walmart or Target. They even sell their toys online to Amazon or on their own website at MelissaandDoug.com. They hire people to help them create new ideas for toys and distribute them to be sold in toy stores. These employees help them serve more parents, teachers, and children.

Some business owners do not have employees and work alone. These people are usually considered consultants or sole proprietors, where they provide valuable information or services to others. An example is a middle schooler or teenager who a starts a lawn service business. They may mow lawns, shovel snow, and rake leaves for people in their neighborhood. The child is then paid by the neighbors after the work is done. This child does not work for anyone, so they can keep the money.

If the child gets more customers, then they may consider hiring other kids as employees to help serve more people. Many business owners start with no employees. Once their business grows, then they may hire help.

Business owners have access to *passive income*, which means their business puts money in their pocket whether they work or not. They don't necessarily have to trade time for money like employees do. For example, the Los Angeles Lakers Professional Basketball team makes money by their fans paying money to see the professional players play basketball. The fans are happy to pay their money because they are entertained at the game. In this case, the owner of the Lakers makes money whether he/she works or not because he or she doesn't have to be on the court playing basketball.

Business owners also have access to portfolio income, which is money made through capital gains. *Capital gains* is when you buy something at a low price and sell it for a higher price than you purchased it. For example, a child may go to the store and buy fifty pieces of candy for $10. Then the child may sell all the candy they just purchased to their classmates for higher prices totaling $25. Therefore, the child's capital gain is $15 because $25 (total amount they made from selling candy) - $10 (total amount they purchased the candy for) = $15 (profit or capital gains).

Business owners do this all the time. The reason they have a business is because they can sell products or services for more than they buy them.

Investor

A third way people make money is by being an investor. An investor is someone who buys items that make them more money. These people study the item they would like to buy in order to know if it is a good investment or not. They are gaining financial education when they study the item in which they would like to invest. Once they have the education, then they develop a plan for how they will invest.

They also have access to passive and portfolio income.

Some investors invest in the stock market, real estate, or other businesses. A person that invests in the stock market buys part ownership in a business. For example, if it costs $100 to own all of Toy World and you pay $50, then you own half of the company, because $50 is half of $100.

When a person buys a stock, they become a shareholder or part owner. Toy World may sell stocks when they create a new product, make an existing product better, hire more employees, or get a bigger building. This is how some businesses raise money. If Toy World sells a lot of toys and their profits go up, most likely their stock prices will increase. In turn, you as a shareholder make money. If they don't sell a lot of toys, then their profits will most likely go down. This means their stock prices go down, which causes the shareholder to lose money. This type of money is called *portfolio income* because the investor is buying low and selling high.

Other investors invest in real estate, which is land or buildings. Let's continue to use Toy World as an example. Toy World has toys in a huge building. However, the Toy World business owner, Michael, does not own the building, Cory does. Cory is a real estate investor because he owns the land and building in which Toy World sells their toys. Therefore, Michael has to pay Cory money every month in order to sell toys in the building. Cory receives this money every month whether he works or not, which is a form of passive income.

Some investors may invest in other businesses. Just like in the stock market, businesses ask investors for money to pay for new products, make an existing product better, hire more employees, or to get a bigger builder. The investor will not give the business their money for free; they want something in return like part ownership in the business or passive income.

Let's say Toy World wants to make one hundred new robots that kids will love to play with. However, they don't have the money to pay to get these robots made. Toy World will ask investors to help them pay for the toy to be made. An investor will agree to give them the money but ask to be paid one dollar for every robot they sell in the future, which is passive income. This type of passive income is called a *royalty payment*. Or that same investor may ask to own part of Toy World. Sometimes, investors ask for both part ownership and royalty payments.

ACTIVITIES

Allowance Time

This activity will teach kids what it means to be an employee.

Materials needed:

- Chore chart (DIY or purchased chart like Melissa & Doug Chore Chart)
- Paper money, or you may use real money if you like

Directions:

- Tell your child you are the owner of a janitorial or cleaning business.
- Create a list of chores for your child.
- You may hold a pretend interview with your child to see if they can perform the chores.
- Tell your child how much you are willing to pay them in play or real money for doing the chores.
- After your child has completed the chores, then pay them with play or real money.
- Discuss with your child what will happen if they are sick and can't do the chore.

- Discuss with your child how they traded time for money in doing the chores.

Career Role Play

This activity will teach kids what it means to be an employee and have a career or job.

Materials needed:

- Written list of jobs or careers, such as a doctor, nurse, engineer, plumber, electrician, firefighter, etc.
- Clothes so the child can dress up as the job or career they choose (optional)
- Play money, or you may use real money if you like
- Make a chart with the seven days of the week like the one below:

Monday	Tuesday	Wednesday	Thursday	Friday	Saturday	Sunday

Directions:

- Explain to your child what each job or career you have listed does to make money.
- Have your child choose what career or job they want to be in your pretend play.
- Have your child dress up as their chosen career or job.

- Make an agreement with your child on how many days per week they will work and the amount they will earn per day.
- Block off days your child will not work or have off.
- Each day have your child dress up in their uniform and create a problem for them to solve.
  - For example, on Monday the problem for a doctor could be a patient has a stomachache.
  - The problem on Tuesday could be a patient hurt his leg while playing soccer.
- Have your child solve these problems in the pretend play.
- Then pay them the amount you agreed upon each day for their work.
- After paying them, have them record it on the chart. An example is below:

Monday	Tuesday	Wednesday	Thursday	Friday	Saturday	Sunday
$10	$10	$10	$10	$10		

- To make this activity more difficult, you may include a scenario where your child hurt themselves or is sick for a day.
  - Discuss how they will get paid. Are they on salary and will get paid regardless? Are they an hourly employee and will not receive money when they don't work?
- You may create a scenario where they get hurt or are sick for a long period of time.

- Discuss what they will do in this situation.

Problem-Solving Activity

This activity will teach kids how to use their ideas to make money for themselves.

Materials needed:

- Child's favorite stuffed animals or action figure
- Paper money, or you may use real money if you like

Directions:

- Tell your child you will play the problem-solving game.
- Create various problems for your child to solve during your pretend play.
  - For example, I created problems for my son and his Black Panther action figures.
  - One problem was Black Panther needed an airplane to save his friend, Nakia, from the bad guys. My son had to figure out how to set him free.
  - So, my son, Cory, built an airplane for Black Panther out of Legos.
- Before your child solves the problem, have them determine how much their services will cost.
- After they solve the problem, pay them in play money.

- Also have your child observe the world and see where they can solve problems.
  - For example, my son's cars kept rolling under the couch.
  - I had to move the couch to get the cars.
  - I told Cory that it was the last time I would get the cars from under the couch.
  - Cory solved the problem by putting pool noodles at the bottom of the couch to prevent the cars from rolling under it.

Cory just built an airplane for Black Panther so he can save his friend, Nakia

Start a Business Activity

Directions:

- Help your child brainstorm various businesses they could start. Some ideas are as follows:
    - Lemonade stand
    - Lawn mowing service
    - Pet-sitting or dog-walking service
    - Jewelry business
    - Create a product like an art supply holder
- Help them get the supplies for the business product or service.
- Have them list their services or products offered.
- Have them set the prices for their services or products.
- Have them market or tell people their idea with the following:
    - Flyers
    - Knocking on doors to tell people about it (if it is safe to do so)
    - Calling family and friends
    - Using social media with parental guidance
- Talk about the importance of doing good work and customer service.

- Once they get their first customer, help them by ensuring they provide good service.

Stock Market Intro

The activity below will introduce your child to the stock market. Because this is an introduction, children will only be able buy one share of stock in this activity.

Materials needed:

- Play money
- Make the chart below

Monday	Tuesday	Wednesday	Thursday	Friday	Saturday	Sunday

- Create a company based on your child's favorite toy.
    - For example, my son loves cars, so my company would be called Fast Cars.
- Tell your child they will be part owner or a shareholder in the Fast Cars Company.
- Give your child $10 in one-dollar bills of play money.
- You will record the following prices for each day in this activity:
    - Monday = $1
    - Tuesday = $3

- Wednesday = $1
- Thursday = 50¢
- Friday = $2
- The stock market is closed on Saturday and Sunday.

- On Monday tell your child the price to own Fast Cars is $1.
- Your child will give your $1.
- You will complete the chart for Monday. It should look like this:

Monday	Tuesday	Wednesday	Thursday	Friday	Saturday	Sunday
$1						

- On Tuesday tell your child the price to own Fast Cars is $3.
- Then give your child $3 so they can see they made money.
- You will complete the chart for Monday and Tuesday. It should look like this:

Monday	Tuesday	Wednesday	Thursday	Friday	Saturday	Sunday
$1	$3					

- On Wednesday tell your child the price to own Fast Cars went down to $1.
- Then have your child give you $2 ($3 - $2 = $1) so they will only have $1.
- You will complete the chart for Monday, Tuesday, and Wednesday. It should look like this:

Monday	Tuesday	Wednesday	Thursday	Friday	Saturday	Sunday
$1	$3	$1				

- Keep going until you get to Friday.
- Discuss with your child how they felt when they lost and gained money.
- Follow a real company's stock prices with your child.
- Pick a company they can relate to such as the businesses that makes their toys or clothes.

Play-Doh Real Estate

Materials needed:

- Play-Doh or modeling clay
- Play money
- Make the following chart:

Monday	Tuesday	Wednesday	Thursday	Friday	Saturday	Sunday

Directions:

- Have your child build a home with Play-Doh or modeling clay.
- Then have your child build two characters (boys, girls, or animals).
- We named our Play-Doh characters Maya and Ryan.

- Allow your child to name the characters.
- Help your child put a price on the home, such as $100.
- Tell your child that Maya is the *owner* of the house because she paid the bank $100 to own it.
- Ryan needs to live in a home, and he asks Maya for help.
- Maya says she will help and provides a home for Ryan.
- However, Ryan will need to pay Maya $5 a month for living there.
- Give Ryan $35 in five-dollar bills.
- Have Ryan pay Maya $5 in January.
- Then complete the chart to show the money Maya is gaining from owning this home:

January	February	March	April	May	June	July
$5						

- A few minutes afterward, say, "Okay it is February and it is time to pay Maya again."
- Have Ryan pay Maya $5 in February.
- Then complete the chart to show the money Maya is gaining from owning this home:

January	February	March	April	May	June	July
$5	$5					

- Keep going until you get to July.

- Discuss how much money Maya has earned in seven months from owning real estate, which should be $35 ($5 x 7 months = $35).
- Discuss people who you know, family, friends, or celebrities, who own properties.

This is our setup for the Play-Doh Real Estate Activity. In the middle is the house. On the right is Ryan, and on the left is Maya.

Investing in Another Business

This activity will teach kids how people invest in other businesses and make money.

Materials needed:

- Legos or any type of building blocks
- Play-Doh
- Play money

- Make the following chart:

Monday	Tuesday	Wednesday	Thursday	Friday	Saturday	Sunday

Directions:

- Have your child build a business with Legos or blocks. Ideas for a business could be as follows:
    - Toy store
    - Indoor playground
    - Skating rink
    - Amusement park
- Then have your child build two characters out of Play-Doh (boy, girl, or animal) named Madison and Bryan.
    - Allow your child to name the characters if you like.
- Tell your child that Madison is the *owner* of the indoor playground called Fun Times.
- Madison wants to build an indoor roller coaster that kids can ride on.
- However, Madison does not have the money to build this new roller coaster.
- She asks Bryan, an investor, for help.
- Bryan agrees to help Madison, but he wants something in return.

- Bryan wants Madison to pay him 50¢ for every child that gets on the ride.

Madison agrees with this.

- On Monday, one hundred kids got on the ride.
- Bryan was paid $50 on Monday because 100 x .50 = $50
- Then complete the chart to show the money Bryan is gaining from investing in Madison's business:

Monday	Tuesday	Wednesday	Thursday	Friday	Saturday	Sunday
$50						

- Below is what happened the rest of the week.
    - Tuesday = 30 kids
    - Wednesday = 50 kids
    - Thursday = 100 kids
    - Friday = 100 kids
    - Saturday = 200 kids
    - Sunday = 150 kids
- On Tuesday 30 kids got on the ride.
- Bryan was paid $15 on Tuesday because 30 x .50 = $15
- Then complete the chart to show the money Bryan is gaining from investing in Madison's business:

Monday	Tuesday	Wednesday	Thursday	Friday	Saturday	Sunday
$50	$30					

- Keep going until you get to Sunday.
- Discuss how much money Madison has earned in a week from investing in Bryan's business.

CHAPTER 5

Budgeting

WHAT IS A BUDGET?

Budgeting is a very important skill that people should possess when handling money. Budgets tell people how much money they earn and spend. It helps people to live below their means or, in other words, not to spend more money than they have. People put their income and expenses in a budget. Expenses are items you buy or spend money on.

What Does a Budget Include?

As previously mentioned, people earn money as an employee, business owner, or investor. These people have basic necessities to pay for in order to live. The basic necessities are usually put in a budget.

These include shelter, food, clothes, children (if they have them), taxes, and utilities. Utilities include items such as water, electric, heating, and gas. Many people include other items that may or may not be considered a necessity, such as savings, entertainment, vacations, and charity.

Why Do People Include Certain Items in Their Budget?

Most people have to pay for the homes they live in. It is difficult to live in a home with no utilities. We need water to drink, to take a bath, and to help clean our home. Also, electricity provides homes with light and energy to cook food in the oven and utilize the fan, air conditioner, and heat.

As humans we have to eat to live, so we go to the grocery store to buy food. Some people grow their own food but may have to go to the grocery store to get food they can't grow. It is against the law to walk around naked in the street, so we have to buy clothes. There are those who make their own clothes, but they have to buy the fabric in order to sew them together.

Taxes are used by the government to pay for items such as public schools, teachers, health care, roads, bridges, sewers, military, and the police. They are based on how much money a person, company, or investment earns. Taxes are also added when you purchase products from a store, like toys, groceries, or hygiene products. They ensure that people contribute financially to how a society functions.

Children are precious but can be expensive. Many working parents have to pay for daycare, food, and clothing for their kids. Furthermore, parents often buy their children toys and take them to fun places like the zoo and amusement parks.

Many people have a moral principle to contribute money to charity. Charities are organizations that provide help and raise money for those in need. Charities can include churches, hospitals, social services, and organizations that help the sick, children, or those who are low income. Some people budget out 10 percent for charity, and some contribute more. In general, it is a great deed to give to others in need.

Two more items included in a budget are entertainment and vacation. It is great idea to relax and plan fun things as a result of working. Entertainment could include going to a movie, sporting event, or the circus, or planning a party. This is a way that people can reward themselves for their hard work. Vacations are when people plan to get away to see different parts of the world. They participate in activities and experiences such as tours, amusement parks, going to the beach, or snorkeling.

Why Incorporating Savings in a Budget Is Important

Another important item to include in a budget is savings. Savings can have many purposes. Having savings helps you work toward buying something in the future. For example, if a child wants to buy a special toy, they can save money they get from Christmas or their birthday in order to purchase it. They may also save money earned from starting a business to buy the toy. Furthermore, people put money in savings in case they lose a job or have to make a big purchase like getting their car fixed. If a person loses their job, it will be difficult to pay for basic necessities. In this case, a person can use money in their savings in order to live.

Living Paycheck to Paycheck

Some people live paycheck to paycheck. This means they have no money left at the end of a month and are waiting for the next paycheck in order to pay their bills. This can be dangerous because if a person loses their job or is sick for a long period of time, they will not be able to pay their bills. For example, if a person makes $1,000 and they spend $1,000 by the end of the month, they are living paycheck to paycheck. The person has to wait to get paid the next month in order to pay their bills. If the same person makes $1,000 and they spend $500, this is called living below your means. This person can save $500 every month, and the money will grow into a bigger amount in the future. The money could be used to buy a business, invest in real estate, or spend when really needed. If enough money is saved over time, it is possible it could be used for all three.

An Important Lesson Budgeting Can Teach Us

A budget can teach us to sacrifice things we want and focus on what is needed. For instance, we may choose to buy an economy car or a less expensive one instead of a luxury car. A luxury car tends to cost more money, and the upkeep is more expensive than that of an economy car. A budget may help us realize that if we decrease the amount of times we eat take-out food, then we could save an extra $200 a month. This money could be put toward savings.

There are times when we want the finer things in life, but our budget does not allow it. The budget may tell us to make more money in order to get the items we want. For example, if you want a more expensive car, then you may have to get an extra job, start a business, or invest in something that will bring passive income in order to get it. For the child who wants a new toy, they may start a lemonade stand to earn money in order to buy it.

Budgets are wonderful tools that can tell us so much about our money! Let's use them for our benefit.

ACTIVITIES

The Budgeting Game

This activity will teach kids the importance of a budget. Children will have a career as a computer programmer. You may change this career and the numbers in the chart if you like.

Materials needed:

- Play money, or you may use real money if you like
- Create a career chart for a computer programmer like the one below:

Computer programmer income	$1,000
Home expense	$400
Utility expense (includes water, gas, electricity, and gas	$100
Tax expense	$200
Food expense	$50
Clothing expense	$10
Charity expense (optional)	You decide how much
Savings	You decide
Entertainment expense	You decide
Car expense	Luxury car for $200 or economy car for $100

Directions:

- Create the chart above for you and your child to see.
- Tell your child they are a computer programmer.
- Computer programmers give computers directions on what to do through writing something called *code*.
- In this activity they make $1,000 a month in their paycheck
- Now it is your child's responsibility to pay their monthly bills.
- Give your child play money totaling $1,000 broken up into $1, $5, $10, $20, and $100 bills.
- Tell your child to pay the first bill, which is their home, at $400.
- Your child will give you $400.
- Next your child will pay the second bill, which is the utility expense at $100.
- They will give you $100.
- Have your child pay the taxes, food, and clothing bills.
- Tell your child they have the option to contribute to charity and they can decide how much.
- (Optional) You may also have your child explain what charity they would like to contribute to and why.
- Tell your child they have the option to put money into savings. They may decide how much.

- Tell your child they have the option to pay for entertainment. They may decide how much and what type of entertainment.
- Tell your child they have to buy a car but can decide if they want the luxury car at $200 or economy car at $100.
- If they have money left over, discuss with them what to do with it.
  - They may put some in savings, buy something they want, or invest in something.
- Discuss with your child what they learned from this activity.

Plan a Meal and a Budget

This activity will teach your child how to budget for your family meals. They will learn the art of adjusting their spending and watching for bargains.

Directions:

- Tell your child they will plan and budget the family meal for a day.
  - You may also have them plan the family meals for a week if you like.
- You will need to assist your child in this activity.
- Tell your child they will have to go grocery shopping for your family and they have a certain amount of money to work with.

- You should determine the amount of money they have for the food budget.
- Have your child plan the meal(s) by drawing a picture or writing a list of the menu.
- You may want to make an initial trip to the grocery store so your child can get an idea of the price for each item.
- Adjust your list or menu after your initial grocery store trip.
- Now it is time to shop.
- At the grocery store, help your child make decisions on what items to get by showing them price-per-unit comparisons.
- Discuss what items are a better bargain.
- Sometimes, you may want to buy the more expensive product.
  - If so, explain why quality may justify a higher price.
- The child's goal is to get the items within the budget.

Budget Scavenger Hunt

This activity will teach your child how to shop for a bargain.

Directions:

- With your child, develop a list of items you need from the store.
- You may create items within a category like the following:

- School supplies
- Clothing items
- Hygiene products

- Take your child to a retail store that has a lot of products or items.
- This activity can also be done on the computer at an online retail store.
- Have your child find all the items on the list at the lowest prices.
- If they see a product that is more expensive, have them justify why they would pay a higher price for it.

Paying Bills

This activity will expose your child to how adults pay bills in the real world.

Directions:

- Tell your child they will help you pay the utility bills.
- Explain that utilities include items such as electricity, water, gas, and trash pickup.
- Explain that utilities help the home run smoothly.
- Go around the house and show your child why electricity, water, gas, and trash pickup are needed.

- Show them that electricity is needed for lights and electronics.
- Water is needed to take a bath, wash the dishes and car, and drink.
- Gas is needed for cooking and heating and cooling the home.
- Show your child the utility bills.
  - You may choose to show them some or all of the bills.
  - Explain various sections on the bill such as the due date, how much was used, the amount, etc.
- Have your child assist you in paying the bill whether it is online or in person.
- Make this a monthly habit if possible.
- You may notice that your child will become conscious of how much energy they use in the home since they know how much it costs.

CHAPTER 6

Basic Banking

WHY DO PEOPLE USE BANKS?

In the previous chapters we discussed the following topics: earning money through a job, owning a business, and investing. We also talked about the benefits of saving your money. Where do most people put their money once it is earned and they want to save it? The answer is banks. American banks are considered a safe place to keep money because if it is lost or stolen, they will give you up to $250,000 of your money back. Many banks are insured by the Federal Deposit Insurance Corporation (FDIC).

When money is given to a bank it is called a *deposit*, which increases the amount of money in your account. Many people put their money in both checking and savings accounts. A checking account allows people to use or have access to their money quickly. Some people use it to pay their everyday bills. People may pay their bills by writing a check, setting up an automatic transfer for the money to be taken out for expenses, or using a debit card. Debit cards allows you to make payments electronically online or by using payment machines in stores. Once a debit card is used, money is immediately withdrawn from the account holder's account.

When expenses are paid through a bank, it decreases the amount of money in your account. You may also go inside the bank to take money out of your account. This is called a *withdrawal*. Withdrawals can also be made at an *automatic teller machine* (ATM). An ATM is an electronic device that allows bank customers to make withdrawals and deposits, transfer funds to other accounts, and check the balance or how much money is in the account.

People tend to like savings accounts because the bank pays you a small amount of money for keeping it there, called *interest*. Interest is usually paid every month. Savings accounts usually limit the number of withdrawals a person makes monthly from an ATM. Generally, you can't make payments directly from a savings account.

An important point is only to spend what is in your checking and savings account. If not, then you will be charged an overdraft fee. When you withdraw more money than you have in your account, the bank will charge you a fee to cover the cost of the transaction. The bank sets these fees, and they can be applied for each overdraft. Some banks have overdraft protection where if you don't have enough money in your checking account to cover a cost, they will automatically get the money from the savings account.

Banks Lend Money

There are times when people don't have enough money saved to buy big items like a house or car. In this case, banks will lend them money to buy these items, which is called a *loan*. However, the bank wants you to pay them back with extra money added to it, called *interest*. For example, if you borrow $20 from a bank, they will give you this amount immediately. When you pay back the $20, they will charge you an extra $2 for giving you the money requested. As a result, you borrow $20 from the bank, but you repay $22.

How Do Banks Make Money?

We know that banks pay you for having a savings account but charge you extra money or interest when you borrow money from them. So how do they make money when they pay their customers money? It is the amount of money they pay customers in relation to what they receive from giving loans. For instance, Jerry deposits $100 in his savings account, then the bank may pay him $1.50 in interest. Then Jackie needs a loan for $200 to start her business. The bank will loan her the $200, but she will have to repay $225. This means Jackie will pay the bank $25 in interest because $200 (amount borrowed) + $25 (interest on loan or amount borrowed) = $225.

Banks also make money from charging fees, like overdraft and overdraft protection fees. They also have a maintenance fee they charge for having a checking and savings account at their bank. When you pay someone or send them money instantly, the bank issues a wire transfer fee. This comes when money is sent to someone and they receive it. Remember we discussed that banks often allow you to make a certain number of withdrawals from a savings account. If you go over that number, there is a fee attached. There are other fees banks charge as well, and this is how they continue to make money.

ACTIVITIES

Check Book Art

This activity will bring out your child's creativity in learning about checks.

Materials needed:

- Art supplies such as crayons, markers, paint, and paintbrush, glitter, stickers etc.
- Scissors
- Glue
- White paper (no lines)

Directions:

- Tell your child they will create a check.
- Explain that a check is a document or piece of paper that tells the bank a specific amount of money to withdraw from one's personal or business account and deposit in another person's personal or business account.
- Show your child a blank check, either one of yours or online.
- Explain the elements on a check and have these included on the check:

- Name and address
- Date
- Check number in top right-hand corner
- Pay to order of (who the check is for)
- Dollar amount line (how much is to be paid)
- Bank name on check
- Memo (what the check is paying for)
- Signature line
- Have your child create a picture of the check.
- Let them be creative in decorating the check.
- Next have them complete the check with your help.
- You may give them a scenario that they will pay $5 to buy a toy or pay the water bill.
- If your child cannot write yet, then have them draw pictures for the following lines:
  - Pay to order of (Draw a picture of who the check is for.)
  - Date (Instead of writing a date, draw a picture of the season; for example, draw leaves for the fall.)
  - For line (Draw a picture of what the check is paying for.)
  - Signature line (Draw a picture of themselves.)
- You, the adult, will complete the rest of the check.

Debit Card Art

Materials needed:

- Art supplies such as crayons, markers, paint, and paintbrush, glitter, stickers etc.
- Scissors
- Glue
- White paper (no lines)

Directions:

- Tell your child they will create a debit card.
- Explain that a debit card comes from a bank and it allows a person to move money electronically to another bank account when buying something.
- Show your child your debit card or a picture of one online.
- Explain the elements of a debit card and have these included on the debit card:
  - Name
  - Expiration date (After this date, you can't use the card anymore.)
  - Debit card number
  - Chip (changes information to data to protect the card and to make sure it is used in the right way)

- Debit card company
- Bank name
- Have your child create a picture of the debit card.
- Let them be creative in decorating the debit card.
- Discuss with your child how and where you use the debit card.
- Once you use the debit card, show your child how the money is taken from your bank account.

Opening Accounts Children's Story
Materials needed:

- Art supplies such as crayons, markers, paint, and paintbrush, glitter, stickers, etc.
- Scissors
- Glue
- White paper (no lines)
- Stapler

Directions:

- Help your child write and illustrate a story about going into a bank and opening a checking and savings account.
- They may staple several sheets of paper together to make a book.

- The story should include the following:
  - Pictures drawn by you and your child.
  - A person going into the bank and opening a checking account.
  - The person should bring money to put in the account.
  - They should also bring photo ID to prove their identity.
  - Tell why they are opening the account.
- Have your child read the story to family members.

How Banks Work Role Play

This activity will give your child hands-on experience in how banks work.

Directions:

- Tell your child they will be the banker and you will play the customer in the role play.
- Have the following happen in your role play:
  - First, you as the customer go to a bank, open up a checking and savings account, and deposit or put money into those two accounts.
  - Second, your child, the banker, pays the customer interest or extra money just for having money in the savings account.

- For example: If David has $100 in his savings account, then the bank pays David $1.50 a year for having the account.

- Third, your child, the banker, uses the money that customers put in their accounts to give out loans.

- For example: If Corrine borrows $100 from the bank as a loan, the bank charges Corrine $12 in interest for borrowing the money.

- Fourth, you, the customer, must go to the bank and withdraw or take some money out of your checking account.

- Fifth, if the bank loses your money, then you can get up to $250,000 of it back through insurance.

- Do this role play in five small increments.
- Once your child understands how banks work, then perform all five increments together.

Open a Bank Account for Your Child

Your child will experience what it's like to open up their own account.

Directions:

- Take a trip to your local bank with your child.

- Ensure they take money they have saved or money you will put in the account.
- Have them observe the environment, like the tellers, offices, etc.
- Help them open up a checking and/or savings account with the teller.
- Have them participate in the process as much as possible.
  - They may give the banker their name, address, and amount to put in the account.
- Have the banker explain the difference between savings and checking accounts.
- Help your child keep track of what is in the account and continue to have meaningful discussions about banks.

CHAPTER 7

Liabilities and Assets

WHAT ARE ASSETS AND LIABILITIES?

I remember hearing the phrase *assets and liabilities* when I was a child. However, I did not have a clear understanding of what it meant. It wasn't until I read the book *Rich Dad Poor Dad* by Robert Kiyosaki that I had a clear definition. He said an *asset* is something that puts money in your pocket, and a *liability* is something that takes something out of your pocket. These definitions struck me because I thought a preschooler could understand them. While playing Monopoly Jr. with my four-year-old, I incorporated these definitions during our playtime. He learned that real estate is an asset. I will go more in-depth in the next chapter.

Asset for One but a Liability for Another Person

One item could be an asset for one person and a liability for another person. For example, the kid buying candy in bulk from the store and selling it for a profit to kids in the neighborhood or at school has created an asset for himself. However, the kids buying the candy have a liability. The candy is an asset for the kid selling it because it is putting money in his pocket. The kids buying the candy are giving their money to the seller, and it is a liability for them.

Once this is understood, then a person may change their thinking about future purchases. I always thought anything of value in a home was an asset, such as a car or computer. I figured you could sell your computer or car and get money from it. However, if you sell your car, you will get less than what you paid for it. For example, if I paid $5,000 for a car, I could only sell it for $1,500 in two years. In this transaction, I am losing money. Buying a used or refurbished computer would have the same scenario as the car. In the past, I have purchased refurbished computers and paid a lower price for them because they were used. In this case, the owner that sold me the computer lost money because he sold it at a lower price than he purchased it.

However, if a person bought a business, then this could be an asset. One of my favorite fast-food restaurants exemplifies this. One of my friends from college purchased a Chick-fil-A fast-food franchise. They serve chicken sandwiches, chicken nuggets, french fries, milkshakes, etc. He knew this would be a profitable business because Chick-fil-A restaurants tend to be full of people. My friend's intuition was correct. Every time you go past his restaurant, especially during lunch and dinner time, it's always full of cars in the parking lot and people in the building. This is truly an asset for him and his family. The people buying food from his restaurant are taking on a liability.

In Real Life

Our world makes it easier and fun to teach kids about liabilities and assets. Let's say you take your child to an amusement park and you see a person selling ice cream. You can talk about how the ice cream is an asset for the ice cream shop owner but a liability for the people buying the ice cream. If you are buying the ice cream for your child, you can explain that life comes with treating yourself sometimes and it may involve buying a liability. It is okay to do this for your entertainment and enjoyment.

Another example would be if you went to the grocery store. You could point out the various companies that sell food in the store. You may pinpoint various brands of apples, cucumbers, tomatoes, or beverages. Explain to your child that having these items in a grocery store is an asset for these brands but a liability for people buying them. However, we need food for nourishment, and this is why the purchase is important.

One option to save money is to grow your own fruits and vegetables in a garden. It is hard work, but if you sell your food at a local farmer's market, it could turn into an asset for you.

My husband and son grew these cucumbers in our backyard.

How Can I Create an Asset?

These conversations may lead to your child asking how they can create an asset. If so, this is great because it will open your child's creativity and get them thinking about how they can use their ideas, gifts, and talents to serve others. If your child comes up with something, encourage them to develop it. This may involve going to the art supply store or hardware store, looking online, or searching for items in your home to develop their idea. Most importantly they will learn in the process and may make money.

One of my son's assets is his creativity and his ability to solve problems. He loves to make up learning games, which I have put in my books and on my blogs. Every time I sell a book he gets money deposited in his piggy bank, which is then put in his bank account. He is already earning passive income at a young age.

Games

One way that I am teaching my four-year-old about the difference between liabilities and assets is through games. One of our favorite games to play is called Cashflow for Kids, which was invented by Robert Kiyosaki, the same man who wrote *Rich Dad Poor Dad*. This game teaches kids the difference between assets and liabilities, how money and investing works, and financial strategies in life. Furthermore, which was mind-blowing, it teaches kids how to complete and read a financial statement. I knew that my son Cory started to understand the difference between liabilities and assets because he was happy when he got to pick up an asset card but sad when it was time to get the liability card.

Cory had mixed feeling when it came to one liability card. It told him to buy a bigger house, which in the game is considered a liability because it kept taking money out of his pocket through monthly payments. He was happy about the bigger house but did not want to make the monthly payment. In the end, he decided he wanted a smaller house so he could pay less money.

Robert Kiyosaki has a host of books and other board games for adults and older children. The games are called Cashflow 101 and Cashflow 202, and they are equally as good as the Cashflow for Kids Game.

Fun In-Depth Learning and Games

If you have read my other books, such as *Teach Your Toddler to Read through Play* and *Fun and Easy Ways to Teach Your Toddler to Write*, you know that I love teaching my son just about everything through fun in-depth learning. *In-depth learning* is being exposed to a concept in various ways. I used the five senses and various learning styles to expose my son to the alphabet, new words, and reading. As you know, the five senses are hearing, seeing, touching, tasting, and smelling. The three basic learning styles are auditory, visual, and kinesthetic. Auditory learners learn by hearing, while visual learners, learn by seeing. My son is mostly a kinesthetic learner because he likes to explore, touch, break apart, and feel what he is learning. However, Cory learns through using all three learning styles and the five senses.

Games incorporate the three learning styles and most of the five senses. Of course, if you are playing a board game, you would not eat or smell the game piece unless you are a very young child. When my son and I are playing Cashflow for Kids, we are discussing our financial decisions within the game. This means we are hearing and listening to what each other is thinking and saying. We are also moving and touching the cards, game pieces, money, and spin wheel in the game. Finally, this game is appealing to children because it is colorful and visually stimulating. The colors help guide my son's learning and make it more appealing to participate.

My son and I playing Cashflow for Kids. He won this particular time we played.

ACTIVITIES

The Difference between Liabilities and Assets Activity

Materials:

- Paper
- Writing utensils like crayons, markers, or pencil
- Make the chart below with two columns: Assets and Liabilities.

Assets	Liabilities

- You may make this more physical by making one sign (instead of drawing the chart above) that says "Assets" and another that reads "Liabilities" and tape each to two boxes, buckets, or bins.
- Ask your child what they would do if you gave them $100.
    - You may give them another dollar amount if you like.
- Your child may say they will buy a toy, clothes, books, or a car.

- Once your child tells you the items they will buy, categorize them under the Assets and Liabilities columns.
    - *For example: If your child would buy a car or toy, then you should put this under the liabilities column.*
    - *If your child says they will start a lemonade stand business, then you would put a drawn lemonade stand or lemon under the asset column.*
- If you are doing this activity with the boxes, buckets, or bins, then have your child draw the items on paper and put them either in the Asset or Liabilities box, bucket, or bin.
- Instead of drawing the products on paper, your child may put a toy, toy car, or clothing in the asset or liability box, bucket, or bin.
- Explain to participants that an asset is something that puts money into your pocket
    - *For example: owning a business and investing in real estate.*
- Explain to participants that a liability is something that takes money out of your pocket.
    - *For example: car payment, buying clothes and shoes, credit card payment.*
- Now tell your child what you would do with $100.
- Have them put the items in either the correct column, box, bucket, or bin.

Liabilities and Assets I Spy Game Activity

Directions:

- While you and your child are running errands, identify assets and liabilities in a fun way.
- Please note that many items can be an asset for one person and a liability for another.
- If your child says an item is an asset, have them explain how this is an asset and who owns it.
- If your child says an item is a liability, have them explain how it is a liability and who is responsible for the expense.
- When you are in a store, go toward a clothing product and say, "I spy an asset."
  - Discuss with your child how this piece of clothing is an asset for the company who made it.
  - You can usually find the company somewhere on the product.
- Then go to another product like painter's tape and say, "I spy a liability."
  - Discuss with your child how this tape is a liability for the person buying it.
- Keep doing this with various items in the store.
- You may also do this activity while you are outside taking a walk.

- If you see a car passing by, you may say, "I spy an asset."
  - Then discuss who the car manufacturer is and how it is an asset for them.

How Can I Create an Asset? Game

Directions:

- Tell your child that people create assets all the time because they want to solve a problem or something needs to be improved, or to fill a need.
- As you and your child are going about your day, observe what people are doing, the various items and products you see, and how things work.
- Challenge yourself to come up with an asset you can create.
- For example, if it is hot outside, can you provide neighbors walking by with cold water.
- If you see kids in a waiting room and they are bored, can you create a fun coloring book to keep them entertained and engaged?
- If you see kids eating snacks while in a store, can you ask the store to put a popcorn machine in there?
- Write your ideas down and execute one of them with your child.

How Can I Turn a Liability into an Asset? Activity

- Tell your child they will practice turning a liability into an asset.
- Let's say you go into a grocery store and see flour and sugar.
- This would be a liability if you used it to make cookies.
- However, if you sell the cookies to family and friends, then it could be an asset.
- If you go into a store and buy a plain cup holder, it would be a liability.
- However, if you decorate it with your artwork and sell the cup holder, then it becomes an asset.
- Continue to do this as you are exploring and going about your day.
- Execute one of your ideas and learn from the process.

CHAPTER 8

Good Debt, Bad Debt

DEBT

Debt is a promise to pay money. Remember in the basic banking chapter I gave the example of Jackie needing a loan of $200 from the bank to start a business. The bank gave her $200, but they required that she pay back $225. This is $25 more dollars than she borrowed from the bank. The $225 that Jackie needs to pay back is called *debt*. The extra $25 added to the $200 is called *interest*. Interest happens when people have debt and they have to pay it back plus extra money. Interest is paid for simply having the debt. This is how the loaner, in this case, the bank, makes money.

Many People Don't Like Debt

There are many people who do not like debt. They hate the thought of owing anyone money and then having to repay it with interest. Many times, owing others money can cause stress and frustration. In some cases, people have too many bills to pay and this leads to debt piling up. When a person has a lot of debt, sometimes they spend more money paying off the interest instead of the actual debt, which also called the *principal*.

For example, my biggest debt in my twenties was my student loans from college. I received these loans from a bank. At one point I owed over $30,000. Whenever I got my bill, I saw the interest number decrease but the principal or debt number remain the same. This was because I was paying the minimum amount or the lowest amount to pay in order to avoid late fees. It took me twelve years to pay it off. I did not see the principal decrease until I started to pay more than the minimum amount.

What Do Some People Do Instead?

Instead of incurring debt, some people choose to save money until they can buy what they want. This tends to take longer, but it gives people peace of mind because either it allows them to have less debt or they are free from owing anyone money. Many people choose to make this process faster by getting another job, which allows them to afford more things. Sometimes organizations like churches or other non-profit organizations will ask for donations from people to help them get a building or purchase products that will help the community.

There are some people who want something immediately but can't pay for it. These people most often choose to use credit cards to buy what they want for instant gratification.

How Do Others Deal with Debt?

The use of credit cards is a way people use debt to make purchases now and pay later. A credit card is a card that lets you borrow money, up to a certain limit, with the understanding that you will repay the bank with interest. People use it to buy things, transfer money, and get a cash advance. A person must complete an application through a credit union or bank to get a credit card. Afterward, the bank or credit union will review the application and check your credit reports. The credit reports help the bank determine whether you will pay the debt back or not. If the credit score is good (700 and above), then a bank will probably think you can repay the money.

One important thing to know about your credit card is the annual percentage rate (APR) and the credit card bill due date each month. The APR is the interest or the amount charged for borrowing money from a credit card. If you pay the credit bill after the due date, you could be charged a late fee. If you continue to miss payments, additional late fees will come, and your interest rate may rise. This results in you paying a lot more money than you borrowed.

One of the major challenges with credit cards is overspending, which is spending more than you can afford. This leads to bills and debt piling up, which can be difficult to repay. Below are some reasons people tend to overspend:

- They want to appear to have a higher income by purchasing luxury items like a big house and expensive cars and clothes.
- They don't want to go without items they want, such as eating out.
- They are addicted to buying more stuff.
- There is no household budget, so they don't know how much money they are spending.

The Difference Between Good Debt and Bad Debt

Some people like debt because they can use it to get assets. In the previous chapter, we discussed the difference between assets and liabilities. Assets are things that put money in your pocket, and liabilities are things that take money out of your pockets. These words can be applied to good debt and bad debt. *Good debt* is when you borrow money to buy an asset. *Bad debt* is when you borrow money to buy a liability.

An example of good debt is when people borrow money to buy real estate or even a business. However, before borrowing the money, you must ensure that the real estate or business can put money in your pocket, because the banks will want you to repay the money. This involves learning about your business to see if people want what you are selling. When it comes to real estate, it is important to ensure your rental income will put money in your pocket.

On the next page are fun activities that will teach your child about debt.

ACTIVITIES

Pay Your Debt Cartoon

Materials needed:

- Art supplies such as crayons, markers, paint, and paintbrush, glitter, stickers, etc.
- Scissors
- Glue
- White paper (no lines)
- Stapler to make a book

Directions:

- Tell your child you will help them create a cartoon about debt.
- You all may draw stick figure characters if you like.
- Your child can name the characters.
- You should draw the following in your cartoon:
  - On page 1, draw a character (Person 1) borrowing $5 from the bank.
  - On page 2, draw the bank charging Person 1 $2 interest for borrowing $5.
  - On page 3, draw Person 1 owing the bank $5 + $2 = $7.

- After making your cartoon, show family members and friends.
- You may choose to act out your cartoon as well.

How Can I Avoid Debt? – Art Collage

Materials needed:

- Art supplies such as crayons, markers, paint, and paintbrush, glitter, stickers, etc.
- Scissors
- Glue
- White paper (no lines) or mini poster board

Directions:

- Explain to your child that debt is the promise to repay money after it is borrowed.
- Along with debt comes interest, which is additional money that needs to be paid with debt.
- Discuss with your child what happened in the previous activity, Pay Your Debt Cartoon.
- Tell your child that some people don't like debt because they don't want to owe anyone money.
- Some people avoid debt by doing the following:
    - Saving their money until they can buy what they want.

- Using an asset to pay for things they want.
- Sacrificing or not buying certain items so they don't need debt.
- It is your and your child's job to come up with ideas of how a person can avoid debt.
- You will make a collage by using art supplies such as follows:
  - Paint
  - Paintbrush
  - Pictures from a magazine
  - Scissors
  - Crayons
  - Markers
- You all may decide to draw or paint pictures and paste them on paper or poster board.
- Cut out pictures from a magazine and paste on paper.
- Examples of pictures to paste on paper or poster board are as follows:
  - Ideas for assets like a business or investment
  - Ideas to save money
  - Items to sacrifice in order to save money
- Discuss and review the ideas with your child.

Credit Card Art

Materials needed:

- Art supplies such as crayons, markers, paint, and paintbrush, glitter, stickers, etc.
- Scissors
- Glue
- White paper (no lines)

Directions:

- Tell your child they will create a credit card.
- A credit card is a card that lets you borrow money, up to a certain amount, with the understanding that you will repay the bank with interest.
- Show the child your credit card (if you have one) or a picture of one online.
- Explain the elements of a credit card and have them included on the picture:
    - Name
    - Expiration date (after this date, you can't use the card anymore)
    - Credit card number

- Chip (changes information to data to protect the card and to make sure it is used in the right way)
- Debit card company
- Bank name
- Card security code—three- or four-digit number located on the back or front of card. Its purpose is to ensure you are the owner of the card.

- Have your child create a picture of the credit card.
- Let them be creative in decorating the credit card.
- Discuss with your child how and where you use the credit card.
- Once you use the credit card, show your child how you must repay the money with interest.
- Show them your credit card statement or a picture of one online and explain how to read it.

Pay Your Credit Card

Materials needed:

- Art supplies such as crayons, markers, paint, and paintbrush, glitter, stickers, etc.
- Scissors
- Glue
- White paper (no lines)

- Play money

Directions:

- Make a colorful, simple credit card statement with markers and crayons on paper with the following items:
    - Bank name
    - Your child's name and address
    - Credit card due date
    - Annual percentage rate (make up an APR)
    - Balance due (make up one)
    - Minimum payment
- Have your child pay the credit card balance with play money.
- Your child may decide to pay the entire balance or the minimum payment.
- Explain what will happen if they pay the entire balance.
- Explain what will happen if they pay the minimum payment.
- Explain what will happen if they don't pay the bill or pay under the minimum amount.
- You may add late fees if they miss a payment or pay under the minimum amount.

The Difference between Good Debt and Bad Debt Activity

- Tell your child they will choose between good debt and bad debt.
- Tell your child the difference between good debt and bad debt.
- Explain to your child that good debt is borrowing money to buy an asset and bad debt is borrowing money to buy a liability.
- Use the Good Debt, Bad Debt Activity box and have your child follow directions.
- The answer key is in the back of the book.
- To make this activity more active, you may draw pictures of each number.
  - For example: Number 1 says: Borrow money for a car wash business or borrow money for a car.
  - Draw the car wash business and car with your child, then discuss which one is good debt.
- If you are playing this game with more than one child, make this a fun game to see who can pick out the good or bad debt first.
- You may give points to the team or child who gets the correct answer first.

Good Debt, Bad Debt Activity

Pick the Good Debt

1. Borrow money for a car wash business, or borrow money for a car

2. Borrow money for clothes, or borrow money for a clothing store

3. Borrow money for a gum ball machine, or borrow money to buy music online

4. Borrow money for a restaurant, or borrow money for candy

5. Borrow money for shoes, or borrow money to start a summer camp

Pick the Bad Debt

6. Borrow money to buy materials to sell paintings, or borrow money to buy comic books to read.

7. Borrow money for a video game, or borrow money for a lawn mowing business.

8. Borrow money to get hair done, or borrow money to buy a hair salon.

9. Borrow money to buy lemonade, or borrow money to buy a lemonade stand.

10. Borrow money to buy shoes, or borrow money to buy a shoe store.

Calculate Good Debt and Bad Debt

- Tell your child they will calculate good debt and bad debt.
- You may create a role play where you are the borrower and your child is the banker or loaner.
- To make it fun, you as the borrower may dress up as different characters, like a doctor, basketball player, firefighter, etc.
- Each time, ask your child to calculate the total amount owed by adding debt and interest.
- You may use the numbers in the Calculate the Debt and Interest box below.
- If your child is younger, use smaller numbers.
- The answer key is in the back of the book

Calculate the Debt and Interest

1. (Debt) $24 + (Interest) $9 =

2. (Debt) $50 + (Interest) $25 =

3. (Debt) $103 + (Interest) $24 =

4. (Debt) $111 + (Interest) $30 =

5. (Debt) $150 + (Interest) $80 =

6. (Debt) $200 + (Interest) $53 =

7. (Debt) $533 + (Interest) $64 =

8. (Debt) $1,055 + (Interest) $432 =

9. (Debt) $2,032 + (Interest) $842 =

10. (Debt) $3,056 + (Interest) $1,477 =

CHAPTER 9

Real Estate

What Is Real Estate?

In Chapter 4 we discussed real estate and how people invest in it to make money. *Real estate* is properties that consist of land or buildings. We need land to live because it provides drinking water, healthy food, clean air, and shelter. It also provides protection from dangerous weather and natural disasters like tornadoes and floods. People need properties such as homes and buildings to live, sleep, meet, play, and conduct work and business. Some people rent properties and others own it, but we all need land and buildings to live.

There are some people who need a place to live, like an apartment or home, but they don't or can't buy it. In this case, they will rent it. This means they will pay money to the owner of the apartment or home every month to stay there. The person renting is called a *tenant*, and the owner is the *landlord*. If something breaks or needs to be repaired in the home, it is the landlord's responsibility to take care of it. In turn, if a tenant is late with paying their monthly rent, then the landlord will charge late fees. If the tenant is late with rent payments continuously, then the landlord may evict them or request the person to leave the property.

Similar occurrences happen when someone owns a *commercial property*, which is a building or land intended to make money. Commercial property often has a lot of people coming and going producing business and making money. Such properties include office buildings, medical centers, hotels, malls, retail stores, farmlands, multifamily housing buildings, warehouses, and garages. The owners of commercial properties want the rent to be paid at a certain time so they can make money.

How Do People Invest in Real Estate?

A person who wants to own property will start searching for them. This involves finding a home, building, or land and looking at it to see if it is something they want to buy. These searches could take months before a potential real estate investor buys a property. Afterward, the person can buy the property by paying a small part of what the property costs or its balance. Then they make an agreement with the bank to pay off the balance and interest, which would be debt to the real estate investor. The investor uses the monthly payment from their tenants to pay off their debt.

As mentioned previously, some real estate investors are landlords who provide housing for their tenants. In turn, tenants pay them monthly to stay in the home. Some people are in real estate investment groups, where a business buys or builds a set of apartments or condos and then allows investors to purchase them through the company. The company usually manages all the units, handles the maintenance, and finds the tenants. Both the real estate investment group and company take a piece of the monthly rent.

Another way people invest in real estate is by *flipping* homes. Flippers typically buy a property and improve it by renovating it. Renovating a property adds value to it. Renovating a property could be painting the walls, getting new appliances like a refrigerator, oven, or dishwasher, and getting new carpet. A property that a flipper buys at $150,000, after renovation, could be sold at $180,000. This has the potential to put more money in the flipper's pocket.

Why Do People Invest in Real Estate?

People like to invest in real estate because they know the amount of money coming into their pockets each month. Real estate investors have expenses like mortgage payment, repairs, and taxes. They add up these expenses and subtract them from the monthly rent they get from tenants. If a real estate investor gets $1,000 from their tenant and their expenses are $900 a month, then their profit is $100 monthly ($1,000 - $900).

Another reason people invest in real estate is because it increases in value. Because land and buildings are so important to human life, property will most likely continue go up in value. Let's say Maya buys a home at $100,000 and decides to move in seven years. In seven years, if she has taken care of her home, she may be able to sell it for $130,000.

Real estate is tax-deductible. Usually real estate investors have to spend money on repairs and property maintenance like mowing the lawn and fixing water leaks. Deductions are expenses the taxpayer has during the year and can be used to help the real estate investor pay less in taxes. The government likes that the real estate investor is providing homes for people, so when they have expenses, they pay less in taxes.

How Do People Make Money in Real Estate?

In the previous section, we discussed how landlords and flippers who provide housing make money. Now let's discuss how commercial real estate investors make money. Commercial real estate investors help our society by providing homes and buildings, but one of the perks is making money. When you go to a fast-food restaurant, someone owns the land underneath it. The owner gets paid rent every month for letting the restaurant be on their land. The restaurant has employees that clean and serve food and customers. The money the restaurant makes from customers is used to pay for employees, food and supplies, utilities, and the landowner. The restaurant needs the building and land so they can have a place to serve customers.

Sometimes, the restaurant owner may also own the land and building.

This cycle also happens with other commercial real estate such as malls and medical centers. Like fast-food restaurants, the mall and medical center are serving their customers. Customers pay money to receive those services. The money made from customers is used to pay for employees, supplies, products, and rent to the landowner. The owners of the mall and medical center buildings take the money to pay the bank, and then what is left over is called *profit*, or money in their pocket.

ACTIVITIES

Everyday Math while at Home

Introduce your child to mortgage or rent payments with this activity.

- Explain to your child that your house or apartment costs money.
- People who live in an apartment pay rent to the owner of the building, called the *landlord*.
- People who own their home usually get a loan from the bank and pay the bank back with interest.
- Your child is going to pay you rent for their bedroom or another room you choose in your home, at the first of each month.
- If you want to get technical, calculate how much your child's room is worth with the formula below:
  - Get a percentage of your child's room by dividing your child's room square footage by the total apartment's or home's square footage.
  - For example, if your home is 1,200 square feet and your child's bedroom is 200 square feet, then their bedroom takes up 16 percent of the home (200/1,200 = 16.666 or 16%).

- Now calculate how much of the rent your child's room represents.
- If your mortgage is $1,600 a month, then your child's rent would be $256 ($1,600 x .16), which is 16% of $1,600.
- If you don't want to get too technical, then come up with a simple figure, like $100, that your child can pay you each month for rent.
- You can have them earn play money daily by doing the following:
  - Paying them a certain amount each day for cleaning up or following the rules.
  - This money can be used to pay their rent.

Play Monopoly but with a Twist

Introduce your child to **investing in real estate** with this game. Use this game to teach your child financial literacy vocabulary such as *assets*, *liabilities*, and *transaction*.

Materials needed:
- Monopoly board game
- If you have a young child, start off with Monopoly Junior.
- There are various versions of this game. The tips below can be used with most versions.

- Player Assets and Liabilities Chart

Player Assets and Liabilities Chart

Player 1 Assets	Player 1 Asset Amount	Player 2 Assets	Player 2 Asset Amount
Player 1 Liabilities	Player 1 Liabilities Amount	Player 2 Liabilities	Player 2 Liabilities Amount

Directions:

- Read the directions on how to play the game.
- Play the game with your child until they start to understand the concept.
- Teach your child the words *assets*, *liabilities*, and *transactions* while playing Monopoly by drawing the Player Assets and Liabilities Chart and writing the definitions on paper.

Assets are things that put money in your pocket, like someone landing on your property and having to pay you money.

Liabilities are things that take money out of your pocket, like you landing on another player's property and having to pay them money. Other liabilities in Monopoly could be paying to get out of jail or paying money for taxes.

Whenever there is money exchanged in the game, like when paying for properties, getting rental income, getting out of jail, or collecting money from the bank, remind your child that this is called a *transaction*.

- Once your child buys a property and someone lands on it, have them write the property name and value on the chart in the asset columns.
- Once your child lands on another player's property, have them write the property name and value in the liabilities columns in the chart.
- In the Player Assets and Liabilities Chart below, another player landed on two of Player 1's properties, Bowling Alley and Pet Store.

Player Assets and Liabilities Chart

- When the other player landed on the Bowling Alley, they had to pay Player 1 $4.

- When the other player landed on the Pet Store, they had to pay Player 1 $3.

- This was an asset for Player 1 because it put money in his pocket.

- Player 1 landed on another player's property, Pizza House.

Player 1 Assets	Player 1 Asset Amount	Player 2 Assets	Player 2 Asset Amount
Bowling Alley	$4		
Pet Store	$3		
Player 1 Liabilities	Player 1 Liabilities Amount	Player 2 Liabilities	Player 2 Liabilities Amount
Pizza House	$1		

- Player 1 had to pay the other player $1.

- This was a liability for Player 1 because it took money out of his pocket.

Let's reiterate what happened in the game:

- Let's pretend your child is Player 1. Your child owns the Bowling Alley at $4 and the Pet Store at $3. If another player lands on the Bowling Alley, then they owe your child $4. If another player lands on the Pet Store, then they owe your child $3.

- Your child had a liability in the game. They landed on another player's property, Pizza House. So they had to pay Player 1 $1.

- Whenever there is money exchanged in the game, like when paying for properties, getting rental income, getting out of jail, or collecting money from the bank, remind your child that this is called a transaction.

- The next player cannot go until all transactions are complete.

- Complete this chart for all players in the game. To see how it is done, please view our YouTube video called "Financial Literacy for Kids While Playing Monopoly" at https://www.youtube.com/watch?v=YiEWdlNGSsY&t=2s.

My son and I learning about liabilities, assets, and transactions through playing Monopoly Jr.

Build Your Investment Property

In this activity, your child will build the house they want their tenant to live in.

Materials needed:

- Building and molding toys like the following:
    - Legos
    - Magnetic tiles
    - Blocks
    - Play-Doh
    - Clay
    - Other art supplies of your choice

Directions:

- Tell your child they will build or mold a house they would like to invest in.
- The house can include the following:
  - Bathroom
  - Living room
  - Bedrooms
  - Basement
  - Refrigerator
  - Oven
  - Pool
  - Garden
- After your child has built the house, have them tell you about their property.
- Discuss with your child why they think tenants will like it.

Fix It

This activity will get your child thinking about what needs to be repaired in the future if they become a landlord.

- Tell your child they own your home.
- You are their tenant.

- Go through your home with the child and see what may need to be repaired in the future.
  - For example, look at the pipes and tell your child there may be a water leak.
  - The heat may stop working.
  - The washer and dryer may need to be fixed.
- Have your child write or draw the list of repairs they come up with.
- Discuss with your child what repairs you have made in the home, and add that to the list.
- Discuss with your child who you would call to fix the issues and their costs.
- Have your child research the cost of various repairs online or by calling local businesses.
- You may also look at videos online with your child on how people repair them.

Commercial Real Estate Investor

This activity will introduce your child to what is needed if they invested in commercial real estate.

- Tell your child that commercial real estate is land or property intended to make money.

- Commercial real estate tends to have a lot of people going in and out of buildings or land to buy products or pay for services.
- In this activity, your child owns their own laundromat and the building where it is located.
- Explain to your child that this is a place where some people go to get their clothes cleaned.
- People have to put coins in the washers and dryers in order for them to work.
- Have your child draw a picture of what is needed in their laundromat to keep customers happy.
- Below are some of the items needed:
    - Washers
    - Dryers
    - Coin machines
    - Laundry carts
    - Detergent vending machines
- Help your child research the laundromat items and their prices on the internet or by calling local stores.
- Optional: take a ride around your local area and find a great location to put a laundromat.
- Optional: visit a laundromat in your local town or city.

Flipper Activity

Your child will be introduced to what it takes to flip a property in this simple activity.

- Tell your child they have just paid $100 to buy a house that needs to be flipped.
- Tell your child that one way to flip a house is to buy it at a lower price, fix it up, and sell it at a higher price.
- Fixing up a house may include doing repairs, painting, and installing new appliances like an oven in the home.
- Your child has a choice of what they will get done.
- They have a budget of $70 to get the repairs and upgrades done.
- Below is a list of repairs and upgrades your child can choose from:
    - $15 for new paint
    - $30 for new appliances (new oven, refrigerator, and dishwasher)
    - $20 for new carpet
    - $35 for new kitchen cabinets
    - $30 for new wood floors
- After they have chosen what they will do to the house, then they will calculate their profit.

- Each item they get done will add double the expense of the item to the value of the house.
    - For example, if they paint the house for $15, then they can add $30 to the house value.
- Your child can add the following value to their home (the prices below have been doubled in value):
    - $30 for new paint
    - $60 for new appliances (new oven, refrigerator, and dishwasher)
    - $40 for new carpet
    - $70 for new kitchen cabinets
    - $60 for new wood floors
- Now they may calculate their new home value (remembering to double the value of the repairs done):
    - If they got new paint and new appliances, the value is now $170 because $100 (price for home) + $30 (new paint) + $40 (new carpet) = $170.
- Have your child draw a before and after version of the home.
- Then they may sell the house to you for the new home value price.

CHAPTER 10

Stocks, Bonds, and Mutual Funds

WHAT IS A STOCK, AND HOW DOES IT WORK?

A *stock* is an investment in a company. When purchasing the stock of a company, you are buying a small piece of the business, called a *share*. The purchaser of the company stock is called a *shareholder*, who is an owner of the company and has the right to share in the profits and vote on the important decisions of the company. The price of that share has the potential to increase or decrease in value based on the financial performance of the company.

Companies issue or sell stock as a way to raise money and grow the business. Public companies sell their stock on an exchange called the *stock market*. Two of the most popular exchanges are the New York Stock Exchange and the NASDAQ. Purchasers of stock, also known as *investors*, can buy and sell (trade) shares via stockbrokers who process the trades.

The stock exchanges monitor the supply and demand of each company stock and post the results in the form of stock prices. These stock prices fluctuate up and down during the day while investors look for opportunities to make a profit from trading their shares.

Some stocks go up and make money while others go down and lose money.

Because stocks have some volatility in prices, they carry a risk of loss but a potential for higher returns on investment. Shareholders can make money from stocks in a variety of ways. We will discuss two:

- When the price of a stock increases in value over the purchase price, the shareholder sells the stock at a profit.
- Some stocks pay *dividends*, which are periodic (mostly quarterly) payments to shareholders as an incentive for owning the stock.

What Is a Bond, and How Does It Work?

A *bond* is a loan to a company or government entity who agrees to pay a fixed rate over a period of time. The investor lends the company or government money for a set period of time with the promise to repay the original money plus interest. This repayment of interest is known as the *coupon rate*.

For example, a $1,000 bond with a ten-year maturity and a 5% coupon rate would pay $50 (5% of $1,000) per year for ten years and pay back the original $1,000 to the investor.

Bonds have risks that are associated with the creditworthiness or ability of the company or government to pay the interest and repay the original investment at maturity.

Bonds issued by the US government are considered one of the safest investments because they are backed by the "full faith and credit of the United States." States, local governments, and corporations also issue bonds that are considered safe. The safety of each bond is graded by ratings agencies such as Moody's and Standard & Poor's (S&P). Bonds that are considered very safe with the higher ratings pay the least amount of interest because there is less risk of losing money.

What Is a Mutual Fund and How Does It Work?

Mutual funds are the combo meals of investing. A mutual fund collectively pools the money of many investors to invest in a group of securities such as stocks and bonds. Portfolio managers are professionals who manage the assets of the mutual fund portfolio. They also make decisions to buy or sell the securities in the portfolio based on the goals of the fund. Although they do not directly own individual stocks or bonds, mutual fund investors share in the profits and losses of the fund's portfolio.

Mutual funds offer immediate diversification in a portfolio to lower the risk and fluctuations in stock market prices because the fund may be invested in hundreds of different investment holdings. The loss in price of one company will have less impact on a portfolio of many companies.

There are a variety of mutual fund types:

- *Stock or equity funds* are the most popular type of mutual funds and invest in a portfolio of company stocks.
- *Bond or fixed income funds* take less risk than stock/equity funds because they are invested in bonds or loans to governments and companies who are rated by agencies.
- *Balanced funds* invest in a combination of stocks and bonds to increase return while lowering overall risk to the portfolio.
- *Money market funds* have the lowest risks and the lowest rate of return because they invest in high-quality short-term investments issued by the US government and large corporations.

Mutuals funds give several opportunities to make money.

Dividend payments are made when a mutual fund receives dividends or interest from some of the holdings in the portfolio. The fund pays that money to investors or reinvests for the investors based on the number of shares held.

Capital gains are achieved when a security has increased in value and the portfolio manager sells the security to realize a profit. These funds are paid to the investors annually.

Increase in net asset value (NAV) is reflected in the share price of the mutual fund. This is very similar to the prices of individual stocks moving higher with the potential to make a profit.

ACTIVITIES

Product and Company Search Activity

This activity will encourage your child to research products they love and know. This activity will lead into the following one, Track Your Stock.

- Ask your child to go around the house and gather products they love and know.
- Take two of those products and research who or what company is its owner.
- Find out if that company is traded on the stock market.
- Keep researching products until you find one that is traded on the stock market.
- For example, Mattel Inc. owns Fisher-Price, which is a toy company.

Track Your Stock

This activity will teach your child how stocks prices go down and up. It will also inform them of how the news can influence stock prices.

Materials needed:

- Play money

Directions:

- You should have found a stock that is traded on the stock exchange by doing the Product and Company Search Activity.
- Now it is time to track stock prices and learn more information about the company.
- You may read headline news about the company and see if you can match it with the prices.
  - For example, if there is big news that the company is creating a new product, will the stock price go up?
  - If one of the company's leaders leaves, will the price go down?
- Give your child play money and pretend you are investing in the company.
- Track the stock price daily for five days to a month.
- You may begin with $100 of play money and buy one share at a time.
  - For example, if Toy World's stock is $25 on Monday, have your child give you that amount.
  - If Toy World's stock goes down on Tuesday to $20, tell your child they have just lost $5.
  - Keep doing this until the end of five days to a month.

- Give your child the amount earned at the end of five days to a month.
- For instance, if Toy World's stock is $35 at the end of five days to a month, then give your child that amount.
- Explain that they have just made $10 in the stock market because ($35 - $25 = 10).

Create Your Savings Bond

This activity will teach your child what is on a savings bond and its meaning. This activity will lead into the following one, The Working Bond.

Materials needed:

- Art supplies such as crayons, markers, paint, and paintbrush, glitter, stickers, etc.
- Scissors
- Glue
- White paper (no lines)

Directions:

- Show your child a real savings bond or a picture of one.
- Explain to your child what typically appears on bonds.

- Denomination – amount paid once the bond has matured
- Owner's name
- Owner's address
- Issue date – when the bond begins to gain interest
- Print date – when the bond was printed
- Series – There are different series of bonds, E, EE, and I. They each have their own rules, interest rates, and features. (Research the different series of bonds together.)
- Serial number is great to have in case your bond is lost or destroyed.

- Have your child create their own savings bond using paper and art supplies.
- Ensure they have all the elements you explained above on their savings bond.
  - Your child may choose one of the following denomination amounts: $50, $75, $100, $200, $500, $1,000.
- They may include a picture on their bond as well.

The Working Bond

This activity will teach your child how a bond works.

Materials

- The savings bond your child created in the Create Your Bond Activity.

Directions

- Your child will learn how a bond works.
- Tell your child they have purchased an EE bond with a five-day maturity and 5% coupon rate.
- Use the denomination number on their bond to determine the cost of the bond.
    - If they have a $100 bond, then they will pay $50 (half the amount).
- Wait until five days have passed to pay them money.
- Use the denomination numbers on their bond to determine the amount owed at the end of five days.
    - For example, a $100 EE bond with a five-day maturity and 5% coupon rate would pay $5 per five days ($5 is 5% of $100) and pay back the original $100 to the investor.
    - The total amount your child will receive in five days is $105.
- At the end of five days, pay them their play money.

Mutual Fund Activity for Beginners Activity

This activity will introduce your child to how mutual funds work.

Materials

- Six stuffed animals or action figures to represent the characters in the scenario
- Play money
- Your child's favorite toy
- Your child's favorite piece of clothing
- Your child's favorite food (this could be a drawing or toy)

Directions:

- Tell your child that a mutual fund collectively pools the money of many investors to invest in a group of securities such as stocks and bonds.
- Tell your child the following scenario.
- Your child would like to invest in stocks, but it is too expensive.
- They need $200 to invest in stocks, but they only have $10.
- Their friend Calvin, is a portfolio manager and tells your child they can invest in a stock mutual fund with $10.

- In this scenario, a portfolio manager is a person that selects the mix of stocks and uses money from other investors to buy into different stocks he/she chooses.
- Calvin says that four other friends have invested $10 of their money in the mutual fund he created, called My Favorites.
- Calvin takes $10 from your child and 4 other friends to invest in the My Favorite Mutual Fund, totaling $50.
- The mutual fund investment started at $50 on Monday.
- By Wednesday the fund went down to $30.
- Your child and the four friends lost $20 ($50 starting investment - $30 value of mutual fund on Wednesday = $20 loss on mutual fund).
- However, they let the money stay in the fund and it went up to $70 on Friday.
- They made $20 by Friday ($70 value of mutual on Friday - $50 starting investment = $20 profit on mutual fund).

Role-Play the Mutual Fund Activity for Beginners Activity

- After telling your child the mutual fund scenario, have them act it out with stuffed animals/action figures and play money.
- One stuffed animal/action figure should represent Calvin, the portfolio manager.
- Four stuffed animals/action figures will be the other investors.

- One stuffed animal/action figure will be your child.
- Give each of the five investors (four friends and your child) $10 in play money.
- Have each of the five investors give Calvin $10 totaling $50.
- Also give Calvin your child's favorite toy, piece of clothing, and food in a pile to represent the My Favorite Mutual Fund he created.
- On Wednesday when the stock mutual fund goes to $30, tell each investor or stuffed animal that if they get out of the investment they will receive $6 each ($30/5 = $6)
- On Friday when the stock mutual fund goes up to $70, have all the investors or stuffed animals cash out.
- The five investors or stuffed animals will receive $14 in play money because $70/5 = $14.
- (Optional) You may make this more difficult and include Calvin's portfolio manager fee.
- Let's say Calvin's fee is $10, then the starting investment would be $40 instead of $50.
- Also, the payout on Friday would be $60 instead of $50. He charged another $10 to process the payout.
- This means each person would receive $12 instead of $15.

CHAPTER 11

Starting a Business

WHAT IS A BUSINESS?

A business is an individual or group of people that come together to make and sell products or services. It usually starts with an idea that people have in their head. There are three major types of businesses: service, distribution, and manufacturing.

A *service business* involves a skill or selling a person's time, like a hospital, because the doctors and nurses have a skill of making people feel better. A *distribution business* is when something is being bought and sold. An example of this would be grocery stores because they buy products from different companies and resell them. A *manufacturing business* is a company that makes something, like Toyota, because they make their own cars.

Business owners are called *entrepreneurs*. Entrepreneurs get their ideas by seeing a need in the world and filling it. Ideas also come from solving problems. For example, if you are in a waiting room with children and many of the kids are asking their mothers for snacks, maybe you could ask to put a snack machine in the room. This way you are helping hungry children who are bored in the waiting room.

A person creates a business to earn profit or make money. The more people an entrepreneur serve, the more money they will make. You, the entrepreneur, that puts a healthy snack machine in a waiting room can charge parents for the snacks. Once snacks are out of stock, then you will put more in the machine. If parents continue to purchase the snacks out of the machine, then you will make money.

Target Market

One of the first things a business owner must consider is their target market. Target market is the customers or people buying the product. You must think about who will be buying the snacks from your machine. In this case, it will be parents and their children. Once you have this figured out, then you must provide your customers with snacks they will buy. This is where research and observation come in handy. This will help you understand what your customer needs or wants.

Market Research

You will find your customers' needs and wants by doing market research. There are three questions you should answer during your research: What do your customers want? Who wants your product? How much are people willing to pay for it? You can do research by observing what children are snacking on in daycares and churches, while in stores, and at the playground, etc. Other answers can be found by interviewing or surveying your target market, which for your snack machine business are parents and children.

An interview happens when you ask people questions face-to-face. Because of technology, you can conduct an interview over the phone or through your computer. People doing a survey write questions on paper and have the person answer them. Again, with technology you can type questions on the computer and send them via email or even through text message and social media.

Business Name

Is it important to have a business name so people can recognize your product and service? There are many ways to pick a business name. You can name the business after yourself or a loved one, like Richard's Snacks. Another option is to name the business after the product you are selling, like Great Snacks. You also may make up a name, like FaSnacks. Let's use the name FaSnacks in this book.

Business Slogan and Logo

A *slogan* is a short memorable phrase that helps customers identify your product or service. For the snack business, the slogan could be "good snacks coming your way" or "snacks that keep you comfortable." The phrase should be quick and give customers a better understanding of your business.

The logo is a drawing or graphic that is connected to the business. Think about the businesses you buy from frequently. Can you see their logo and automatically name the company? Most people can do this for big companies like Nike shoes. Their swoosh sign is one of the most popular logos in the world. The logo for FaSnacks could be a picture of a child eating a good snack. It could also be a picture of a bunch of snacks in a basket. You want people to be able to look at your image and name your business. This is a great time to be creative.

Business Concept and Unique Features

Every business has a concept and something unique or different that sets them apart from others. A business concept is what your product or service is doing for people. For example, businesses that make toys create a product where children can use their imagination, be creative, and play. A great concept for FaSnacks could describe the benefits of healthy snacking for kids. The concept can be FaSnacks prevents hunger and provides energy, protein, vitamins, and minerals for kids in a fast manner.

Next, you have to figure out what is unique about your business. There are many snack machines in the world today. So why would anyone choose your snack machine over another one? One thing you could do is have colorful characters on the snack machine that draw kids' attention. Also, many machines have unhealthy snacks full of sugar and salt. Most parents want to give their children food that is healthy and nutritious, like what you offer at FaSnacks. Another way to stand out is to have an inspirational message on the snacks. The message could read, "You are strong and brave."

Products

Now that you know your business name, slogan, logo, concept, target market, and the type of snacks parents and children want and need, it is time to purchase your products.

Please note: There are a lot of things to think about when it comes to a business. It is great to answer these questions in the planning stage, but sometimes the best way to solve the problem is to start the business. Once you start, you will answer the questions as you go along.

Make a list of what you need to purchase. FaSnacks will need a snack machine and snacks. You may want to include healthy drinks such as water and fruit juices. There are important questions you should be asking yourself. Will you get a used snack machine or a new one? What snacks will you put in the machine? Examples of healthy snacks are baked chips, fruit cups, and nuts. How much product will you need to fill a snack machine?

Another question to ask is this: How will you get the money to buy the product? It could be from the money you saved from your job, chores, or birthday and Christmas gifts. You may get a loan, which is debt. Remember, you most likely will have to pay interest on your loan. Another option is to get someone to invest in your business. The business investor may give you the money for snacks, but most likely will want something in return, like for you to pay them 5¢ for each snack you sell.

Other Things to Note for Your Product and Business

Below is a list of questions to think about for FaSnacks:

- How often will you visit the FaSnacks machine to check the stock or number of snacks?
- Who will clean the machine?
- Who will repair the machine once it is broken?
- Will you pay the building owner rent for having your snack machine in one of the rooms?
- Who is your contact person for the waiting room?

Business Competition

Most businesses have competition, which is when two or more companies are selling the same or similar products. An example would be two sport apparel companies that are popular in the United

States: Nike and Under Armour. It is similar to when two professional basketball teams are playing against each other. They want to know the strengths and weakness of the other team. Similar to basketball, competing businesses develop ways to beat each other by drawing more customers to themselves.

So, think about FaSnacks' competition. Who would it be? If you were sitting in the waiting room where the snack machine was housed, you may be able to see the competition before your eyes. Your competition may be the snacks parents brought from home. It could be the brand of baked chips or water they are consuming while waiting. It could be another snack machine on the upper or lower floor. Your competition may be also be the convenient store full of snacks on the way to the waiting room's parking lot.

How would you stand out from the competition? This goes back to your business concept and what makes you unique. Remember, you have colorful characters on your machine and personal messages on your snacks. Furthermore, you save parents time from going into a grocery store because the location of the machine is in the waiting room.

Marketing

Marketing is how you will tell others about your business. You don't have a business if people don't know about it. Kids market all the time. When a child has a birthday party, they give their friends invitations. Many schools and non-profit organizations that serve kids have fundraisers like car washes. Children will create posters and stand near the road so people will know about their event. Additionally, kids will create flyers and give them to customers going into a shopping center. These are great ways to advertise a business.

There are other ways to market your product. One way is word of mouth, which is passing information about your business from person to person through talking or reading. If you have a great product or service, then people will tell others about it.

Media is a great way to reach a lot of people. This includes radio, television, magazines, telephone, and the internet. Many of us have seen news and talk shows interview entrepreneurs. The host interviews the business owners, and this provides great exposure for the company. Also, the internet is the fast way to advertise a business. People do this through videos on YouTube, advertisements on social media platforms like Facebook, and podcasts.

When marketing, ensure your advertisement is appealing to the customers. FaSnacks may show a video of a child who is bored and irritable from being in the waiting room too long. However, after their parent gets a snack from the machine, they are calm, happy, and comfortable.

The more you market and people know and like your product, the more people you serve.

Finance

In most cases when starting a business, you need money. The money needed to start a business is called seed money or start-up capital. You will need to make a list of what is needed for your new company. In the FaSnacks business, you will need to pay for vending machines, snacks and drinks, and marketing. If you borrow money from someone to buy the vending machine, then you will have to pay the debt back. You may also choose to have a business investor or venture capitalist to invest in your new business. Marketing costs may include buying posters, paper, and art supplies for flyers. Many magazines and radio shows charge to advertise on their platforms. Furthermore, some people pay for advertisement on social media outlets like Facebook.

There are also ways to cut your start-up costs. In the FaSnacks business, you may find a used vending machine online or a free one. However, you must check the quality of this machine to ensure it is working properly. You don't want it to break down when customers are purchasing your snacks. You can go to a wholesale store that sells snacks in bulk. You may be able to buy thirty packs of chips in one box and then sell them to your customers individually.

Utilizing social media is a great way to cut marketing costs. Children, with their parents' oversight, can share a post about their business to family and friends. Many times, family and friends will share this information, which is more advertisement for the business.

You will need to account for miscellaneous costs such as machine repairs, artistic work done on the machine (optional), gas to and from the waiting room to fill the vending machine, etc.

Money Coming In and Out

You will also need to keep track of the money coming in and out of your business. The best way to do this is through an income statement. This statement tells the business owner whether they made or lost money. When you make money, it is called a *profit*, and when you lose it, it is a *loss*. There are two income statement formulas:

Sales	Cost of Goods	Gross Profit
(How much money you made)	(How much it costs to make the product)	(How much money is left after selling, buying materials, and making the product)
Gross Profit	Other Expenses	Net Profit
(Money you have left after selling and buying supplies)	(Other money you have spent)	(Money you have left after all your spending)

Let's go over an example below. You will complete a financial statement for one month. As a business owner starting out, you may not make money. You have to be patient until you figure out your market and product.

You are the business owner of FaSnacks. It costs you $100 to purchase a vending machine and an additional $50 for snacks. Your mother gave you a no-interest $100 loan for the machine. You have to pay her back $5 each month. You decide to save money on marketing by posting your new business on social media. During your first month, you make $200 in sales.

Here is your sample financial sheet:

FaSnacks Income Statement

Sales/Revenue (*Price of Product x How many you sold at sales event*) **$200.00**

Cost of Goods *(How much it cost you to make the item)*

Item 1 **Vending Machine = 100.00**

Item 2 **Snacks = $50.00**

Item 3 _____

Item 4 _____

Total Cost of Goods (Add item 1, 2, 3, and 4) **$150.00**

Gross Profit *(loss) (Sales - Total Cost of Goods)* **$50.00**

Other Expenses (Other money you spent)

Marketing **$0.00**

Loan Payments **$5.00**

Rent **$0**

Salaries/Pay **$0.00**

Taxes **$0.00**

Other Expenses **$0.00**

Total Other Expenses $5.00

Net profit *(loss)* *(Gross Profit - Total Other Expenses)* **$45.00**

ACTIVITIES

The activities below will help your child plan their new business idea in a fun and imaginative way. Take these activities in small steps, preferably one day at a time.

For all the activities below, you will need the following:

- Paper
- Pencil
- Markers
- Crayons

Brainstorm Your Idea

This activity will help your child create a list of business ideas they can pursue.

- Encourage your child to make a list of items that answer the three questions in this section.
- You could answer the questions by doing the following:
    - Writing the answer
    - Drawing a picture of the answer
    - Building the answer with Play-Doh, blocks, etc.

- Or even more creatively by creating an interpretive dance for your answer
- The questions are as follows:
  - What is something you can help people with?
  - What is a problem you can solve for others?
  - What is something you can improve upon or make better?
- Reference thirty kid business ideas at the end of this chapter.

Who Is Your Target Market?

This activity will help your child figure out the target market for their idea.

- Remind your child that the target market are the customers or people buying the product.
- The target market could be any of the following:
  - Children
  - Adults
  - Business owners
  - People who love to read
  - People who love to dance
  - Any person your idea could help or benefit

- Have your child make a of list of their target market by doing one of the following:
  - Writing the answer
  - Drawing a picture of the answer
  - Building the answer with Play-Doh, blocks, Etc.
  - Creating a dance
  - Creating a role play to reveal the list (but ensure it is written down)

The Search – What Materials or Supplies Do You Need?

This activity will help your child determine the materials needed to make their product:

- Once your child has settled on a business idea, have them create a list of supplies needed to make their product or do their service.
- Encourage your child to do a hunt around your home to find supplies needed in their business.
- You may also contact family members and friends to help gather materials.
- Do a search on the internet for other supplies you need.
- Make a list of your findings and their costs.
- Your child could write or draw out the list.

Make a Prototype or Do the Service for Free

This activity will help your child determine if the product or service they offer is useful or helpful.

- Once your child has gathered supplies, have them make a prototype.
- A prototype is a sample of your product.
- If you are starting a T-shirt business, then make a sample shirt and wear it.
- See if your family and friends like the shirt.
- If you are starting a lawn care business, cut your neighbors' grass for free and see if they like your service.
- Have family, friends, and neighbors give you feedback on the product or service.

Create a Business Name, Logo, Slogan

This activity will help your child create a name, logo, and slogan for their business.

- Encourage your child to brainstorm a name for their business.
- Some ways that people create names are as follows:
  - Using their own name or a family member's name
  - Naming the business after the product; for example,
    - Creative Bracelets

- They can also draw inspiration from the outside world.
- Tell your child a slogan is a short memorable phrase that helps identify the business, product, or service.
- A slogan for Creative Bracelets could be "We Make Your Wrist Shine."
- Help your child create a slogan for their business.
- A logo is a drawing or graphic that is connected to the business.
- Have your child draw or build their logo with art supplies and building toys.
- Next time you are running an errand, identify logos and slogans of clothing, grocery stores, and restaurants.

What Is Your Business Concept?

This activity will help your child figure out what is unique about their business.

- Encourage your child to think about what they see their business doing for people.
- Will their business help people save time, feel good, or look fashionable?
- What is different about their business?
- Do a role play with your child where you are the interviewer and they are the interviewee.

- Ask them the following questions:
  - What is your business idea?
  - How will your business help people?
  - What is different about your business?
- Write down your child's answers (or you may have them write or draw them) and add it to their business plan.

Who Is Your Business Competition?

This activity will help your child analyze similar businesses.

Materials needed:

- Twenty index cards for each person

Directions:

- Tell your child that most businesses have competition.
- Business competition is when two or more businesses are selling the same or similar products.
- Competing businesses develop ways to draw more customers to themselves.
- Play a simple game with your child, like Card High, to show them what competition is.
  - Card High involves giving twenty index cards to each player.

- Bend and twist cards to make the highest building in five to ten minutes.
- The person with the highest building wins.
- Imagine that the person with the highest building will draw more customers to their business because they are most visible.
- You may borrow strategies from the other person in the game to build a higher building.

- Encourage your child to think of other businesses that are similar to theirs.
- Have them write, draw, or tell you what is different and similar about their business.
- Have your child communicate how they plan to draw more customers to their business.

Market Research

This activity will help your child learn what their customers need and want in a product or service.

Materials needed:

- Paper
- Pencil
- Art supplies

- Telephone
- Computer (optional)
- Smartphone (optional)

Directions:
- Tell your child that market research gets your potential customers or target market to answer the following questions:
  - What do your customers want?
  - Who wants your products or services?
  - How much are people willing to pay for them?
- In order to answer the questions above, you have to do market research.
- Market research includes the following:
  - Surveys – asking people questions on paper, through email or telephone, or online
  - Interviews – asking people questions face-to-face
- Help your child create market research for their business by using questions similar to those in the beginning Market Research Activity.
- Your child could do the following:
  - Create a survey to email or give to people.
  - They may also call people and ask them the survey questions by phone.

- Schedule an interview with family and friends.
- They could post questions on social media with a parent's guidance.
- They could make their survey and interview questions colorful by decorating them with art supplies.
- Once your child has created their market research questions, have them survey or interview their target market.

Finance and Your Business

This activity will help your child think about the money needed to start their business.

Materials needed:

- Paper
- Pencil

Directions:

- Now that your child has developed their idea and knows who their customers are, it is time to think about the business finances.
- Help your child make a list of supplies they will need to make the product, do the service, market the business, etc.
- Beside the items needed, help your child research their costs and record this on paper.

- Brainstorm with your child how they will get the start-up money. Examples are below:
  - Doing chores to earn the money
  - Doing a service for others to get money, such as making and selling bracelets
  - Getting a loan from family and friends (Remember, you will need to pay interest.)
  - Getting a business investor to invest in the business (They may want money from your sales in the future or part ownership in the business.)
  - Using money they received as gifts
- Next, help your child purchase the materials needed to start their business.

Market Your Business

This activity will help your child tell others about their business idea.

Materials needed:
- Poster
- Card stock paper
- Art supplies
- Telephone
- Computer (optional)

- Smartphone (optional)

Directions:

- Tell your child that marketing means telling others about their business.
- Ask your child how they found out about their favorite toy or food.
- Ask and brainstorm with your child how they plan on telling others about their business.
- Various ways to market a business are as follows:
  - Commercial
  - People seeing your products in stores and see you doing the service
  - Flyers
  - Posters
  - Phone calls
  - Website
  - Social media
  - Radio
  - Magazine
  - Postcards
  - Business cards

- You want to include the following on your marketing materials:
  - Business name
  - Contact name and phone number
  - Email address
  - Website (if you have one)
  - Logo and slogan
  - Services and product selling
  - Cost (optional)
  - How it will help or benefit customers
- Help your child make marketing materials for their business.
- They could do one of the following:
  - Make flyers, business cards, or postcards with poster, cardstock paper, and art supplies.
  - Create a commercial with a smartphone or video camera and post to social media with parental guidance.
  - Make phone calls to family and friends.
  - Call or research local magazines and radio stations and inquire about how to create an advertisement with them (this may cost money).
  - Ask your child to come up with more ways to market their business.

- Once your child has created their marketing materials, put it out to the world.

Manufacture or Do the Service

This activity will encourage children to serve their customers with their product or service.

Directions:

- After marketing their business, your child may get their first customer.
- This is the time to manufacture the product or do your service.
    - Depending on your business, it may be better to do this step before marketing.
- Encourage your child to make the best product they can or do the service to the best of their ability.
- You want to provide excellent work so your customers will give positive reviews to others.

Customer Service

This activity will teach your child how to make their customers happy and keep them coming back for more:

- *Customer service* is when a business gives good service to a customer and treats them well.
- Examples of good customer service skills are as follows:
  - Answering a customer's question politely
  - Helping the customer to solve problems
  - Replacing a bad product
- Do a role play with your child dealing with customer service.
  - Pretend you are a potential customer wanting to buy something from your child's business.
- During the role play, remind your child to do the following:
  - Greet customers in a pleasant manner.
  - Find out the customers' interest in the product or service.
  - Answer questions clearly.

Time to Sell

- Encourage your child to have fun.
- Forewarn your child that some people will not buy their product or service.
- Encourage your child to keep telling people about the product through passing out marketing materials, posting on social media, or using word of mouth.
- Tell your child that more nos from customers leads to more yeses.

- This trains kids to have courage when people say no.
- It also encourages kids to keep asking more and more people.
- Keep the money you have earned in a safe place.
- Learn from your mistakes and solve the problem.
- Keep doing what worked well in your business.

Financial Statement

- It is important to keep an account of the money you made or lost with a financial statement.
- Help your child complete the financial statement below.
  - You may complete the statement biweekly or monthly.

Income Statement

Sales/Revenue (*Price of product x how many you sold at sales event*)

_____

Cost of Goods *(How much it cost you to make the item)*

Item 1 _____

Item 2 _____

Item 3 _____

Item 4 _____

Total Cost of Goods (Add item 1, 2, 3, and 4) _____

Gross Profit *(loss) (Sales–Total Cost of Goods)*

_____

Other Expenses (Other money you spent)

Marketing _____

Loan Payments _____

Rent _____

Salaries/Pay _____

Taxes _____

Other Expenses _____

Total Other Expenses _____

Net Profit *(Loss)* *(Gross Profit – Total Other Expenses)*

_____

30 KID BUSINESS IDEAS

1. Jewelry designer
2. T-shirt designer
3. Game creator
4. Dog walker
5. Baby sitter
6. Pet sitter
7. YouTube personality
8. Face painter
9. Author
10. Musician
11. Magician
12. Lawn care provider
13. Errand runner
14. Tutoring service
15. Candler maker

16. Baker

17. Graphic designer

18. Party planner

19. Resell merchandise

20. Artist

21. Balloon artist

22. Sell custom designed picture frames

23. create greeting cards

24. Lemonade stand

25. Car washer/detailer

26. Clothing designer

27. Sell bottled water

28. Creating gift baskets

29. Photographer

30. Cleaning service

CHAPTER 12

Field Trips and Real-World Activities

A LITTLE NOTE FROM ANDREA

One of the best ways to have children learn a new concept is through experience. Field trips provide real-world experiences and heighten their understanding of the world. They provide connections between what they are learning at school or home. Furthermore, on field trips, children are encouraged to think about how to solve problems they see in the world and have a direct impact.

In this chapter, we are going to discuss financial literacy field trips. These trips will give your child a broader understanding of how money works, is circulated, and is utilized. You will be able to do these activities with your child on your time and provide them with a fun, in-depth understanding of money.

A Little Note from Linsey

As a financial consultant and creator of interactive financial education experiences, I enjoy the learning that takes place when children experience financial concepts, terminology, and strategies firsthand. You don't have to be a financial professional to begin teaching your children financial literacy. In fact, you are your child's first financial advisor and educator. The financial transactions your child observes you making can greatly influence your child's financial future.

Look for opportunities during your daily routines to engage children in financial and business transactions. Below are some examples that you can use to create memorable experiences. Some of these I still remember from my childhood.

Financial Transactions During Meals

When ordering a meal at a restaurant with a cashier, give the child cash to make their meal purchase. Make sure they have more cash than the cost of the meal. Allow them to approach the counter alone and interact with the cashier by ordering their meal, exchanging cash for their order, and receiving change. After receiving their meal, ask if they got what they ordered.

A few tips to prepare the child for making their meal purchase are as follows:

- Discuss what the child wants to order and make sure they identify the total cost for their meal (drink, dessert, etc.).
- Ask them how many dollars are needed to buy their meal.
- Remind them to wait for their change after giving their money to the cashier.

- Do a practice run allowing the child to tell you what they plan to order.

Financial Life Lessons & Teachable Moments

There may be an occasion when the child does not receive the correct change when paying for an item. In this instance, discuss with the child the correct change due. Then, instruct the child to go back to the counter and inform the cashier that they did not receive the correct change and ask for the correct amount. Be there to support the child, but allow the child to talk with the cashier directly to correct the issue.

During the first experience, you and the child will both be nervous, but after a few attempts your child will feel very confident communicating with adults and handling everyday basic financial transactions when making a purchase.

In another scenario, you can set a spending limit that requires the child to decide about what items they can afford with the money you've provided. For example, the child may have to order the free cup of water rather than a non-free drink to fit within their budget.

Try these suggestions with your students or children and continue the financial life lessons and teachable moments!

Financial Transactions at Financial Institutions

On your next trip to the bank, allow your child to make the deposit or withdrawal with the teller. Instruct the child to tell the teller that they would like to make a deposit or withdrawal to or from the checking or savings account. The teller will be very impressed with your little financial guru as they process the deposit and give the child the transaction receipt. Let the child know the teller may ask, "Is there anything else I can help you with today?" The child should respond to the teller's question and also say thank you.

Financial Life Lessons & Teachable Moments at the Bank

Take your child to open a custodial bank account. Discuss what it means to have a custodial bank account and the opportunity you are providing them by having their own account. Allow the child to make deposits and withdrawals, as appropriate, at the bank on a regular basis. This will help your child develop the confidence and the responsibility of transacting business with financial professionals.

As a parent, teacher, or guardian, you should always look for opportunities to make everyday activities educational experiences to increase your child's financial literacy. Don't let your child be a passive participant in life before they begin making financial and business decisions without thirteen or more years of previous experience.

A few tips to make the banking field trip more meaningful:

- Have your child observe the bank employees such as the tellers, bank managers, and customer service representatives.
- Explain their roles and how they are helping customers.
- If time permits, have the employees explain their roles to your child.

Financial Trip to Pay Bills

As a child, I remember paying bills with my mom monthly. I would sit down at the kitchen table or in the car, look at the utility bills, and write checks to pay them. My mom would sign them and explain to me the purpose of each bill. We would go into each building where the bill was due and pay it. Sometimes, but rarely, she would mail the payment off. I think it made her feel better to deliver the payment herself. It gave me a better appreciation of how my parents provided for us as a family.

You can do this same activity with your child. When they see there are separate bills for the lights, gas, water, trash pickup, and other household expenses, have your child write checks and money orders for the bills. If you pay your bills online, have them observe this process.

Other bills your child can observe you pay are as follows:

- **Mortgage payment** – explain how the bank helps you pay for your house by loaning you money. Don't forget to discuss how you must repay the debt to the bank with interest included. Also show your child the mortgage bill and where the interest and principal amounts are located.

- **Credit card bill** – explain the purpose of a credit card. Credit cards help you purchase items faster. Review that a credit card is considered debt that must be repaid with interest.

- **Cable and internet bills** – explain that cable and internet provide entertainment for the family. However, many people use the internet for work. If you have other purposes for having cable and the internet, explain that as well. Review the services you are paying for and the bill amount.

- **Cell Phone Bills** – explain that cell phones help you communicate with others and research information (if you have a smartphone). Many people use cell phones for work. Explain the services the cell phone company provides, like texting and internet. Also review the bill amount.

Please note: In all your bills, pinpoint the taxes you have to pay. Review with your child what taxes pay for, such as roads, schools, and healthcare. Also discuss the due dates and what happens if you pay a bill late.

Financial Trip to the Grocery Store

Many of us go to the grocery weekly or biweekly because we need food to live. Why not create a powerful financial literacy lesson from this?

Let your child plan the meal for the day. First, they should think about what the family likes to eat. They can interview family members and make a list. Next, have them come up with estimated costs for each item by looking online or in the newspaper. Help your child determine a total estimated cost for their items. Finally, go shopping with your child to purchase the items. If possible, have your child pay the cashier for the groceries and have them count their change. You may also allow them to scan the food in the self-checkout aisle. Remember to keep the receipt. When you get home, prepare the meals and make a list of what the items actually cost.

More tips for going to the grocery store:

- Take a calculator to keep track of the costs as you are putting the groceries in your shopping cart.
- Discuss with your child how you compare which brand or category of certain items you buy.

- For example, do you buy organic store fruit? Why or why not?

Financial Trip for a Major Purchase

A major purchase includes buying a more expensive item such as a car, television, oven, computer, piece of furniture, or washer or dryer. When you are buying these types of products, take your children along to observe the process. They will have more of an appreciation for the item. Have your child observe the conversation between you and the salesperson. If you are making the purchase online, discuss with your child what you are looking for in that purchase. If this purchase requires you to take out a loan, ask the financial counselor if they can explain to your child how they help people buy expensive items. Also have the financial counselor explain the benefit to you as the customer and their company.

Other tips for teaching your child about making big purchases are as follows:

- Explain to your child that good credit (score above 700) tells lenders you are responsible with money.
- With good credit, you are more likely to get the product or service you want with less money.
  - You may get a larger loan amount with a lower interest rate.

- If time permits, have the financial counselor explain to your child what good and bad credit means.
- Ask your child's opinion about the purchase and whether it is best to pay with cash or take out a loan.

Favorite Restaurant

Many kids love to eat at restaurants. The combination of good food with the atmosphere of people socializing provides a great experience for kids. While you are in the restaurant, discuss the financial aspect with your child. Tell your child that the restaurant is a business that started with an idea. There is an owner that is responsible for paying the servers, hosts, and cooks. Also, restaurant supplies and ingredients must be purchased, such as the utensils, plates, tables, food, uniforms, pots, pans, etc. Explain to your child that someone owns the building in which the restaurant is housed. The business owner may own the property. If not, the owner pays rent to a landlord, who owns the building. The building owner does not need to be at the restaurant, they just get paid rent. The restaurant owner is relying on customers to pay for supplies, employees, and rent.

Other tips for restaurant field trip:

- Challenge your child to look around the restaurant and list what other items the business owner is responsible for.

- Ask your child whether they think the restaurant location is good for business. Why or why not?
- If they were the business owner, what would they do differently?
- If they were the building or landowner, what would they do differently?

Field Trips to Apartment Building:

While riding around our city, I am always seeing construction sites where they are building new apartments. This provides an excellent opportunity to discuss with your child how apartment owners make money. You may also do this with existing apartments in your area. When you see an apartment building, tell your child that the people who live there are called *tenants*. Tenants pay rent to landlords or apartment owners. Rent payments allow the tenant to live in one of the apartments. Some landlords offer extra items, such as a laundry room, tennis court, workout room, and pool.

The tenant has a certain time of the month to pay rent. If they are late, then most likely they will pay a late fee. If the tenant continuously misses payments, then the landlord may evict the tenant or ask them to leave.

Other tips for apartment building trips:

- Ask your child why they think people would rent an apartment instead of buying a home.
- Discuss with your child why someone would want to own an apartment or be a landlord?
- Discuss some of the problems the landlord needs to solve, such as repairs and late payments.
- Ask your child what they would provide if they owned an apartment.

Business Owner

Businesses are helpful to our society because they provide products and services we need and want. They also solve our problems, improve upon existing services and ideas, and make our lives easier. In your city, town, or neighborhood, there are bound to be a number of entrepreneurs making our society better.

A great activity is to have your child talk to business owners and interview them. Take a trip to their place of business and find out what they do on a daily basis. Some of the questions your child can ask are as follows:

- How did you come up with this idea?
- How did you get the money to start your business?

- How many employees do you have?
- How do you find your employees?
- How do you find your customers?
- What is the best thing about being a business owner?
- What is the worst thing about being a business owner?
- Have your child create their own questions.

Bonus tip: If your child is really interested in what the business owner does, they can offer to work for the entrepreneur for free. This would be a valuable learning opportunity for your child. They can get the inside secrets of what it takes to be a business owner.

Field Trip to the Future

Have you ever asked a kid what they want to be when they grow up? A typical answer to this question may be a veterinarian, fireman, doctor, or astronaut. How about asking a kid to share their ideas for new inventions or ways to solve problems? A child may have an idea to make their chores easier by inventing an automatic bathroom cleaner.

When a child answers these questions, why not take a field trip to the future! For the child who is interested in animals, schedule a field trip to the zoo and meet a zoologist. Ask your local veterinarian if your child can visit with them for a moment. Another idea is to take a nature walk and make observations about animals.

The child who wants to invent the automatic bathroom cleaner will have to work in smaller steps. They may begin by observing the janitor at their school. Cleaning a bathroom can be a big task, so maybe they can start by creating the automatic toilet cleaner. The next step may be for the child to draw their invention on paper and decide what materials are needed. Afterward, take the child to a hardware store to decide, view, and purchase materials needed to make a prototype of their idea.

Another way to stimulate a child's imagination is to visit the local library to read about people who share your child's interest. Having children read biographies of people who have changed our world will encourage your child to dream, invent, and be imaginative. An internet search is also very helpful to get more information about our world's innovators!

The point is to expose your child to real-life examples that match their interests! It can be fun and is a way to keep your child's brain active.

Field Trip About Stock Market or Mutual Funds

A great way to introduce your child to the stock market is to take a field trip to a trading room at a local college or university. A number of colleges now offer live trading rooms on campus that feature a large ticker tape and big-screen televisions broadcasting the financial news channels. Many of the trading rooms will also feature rows of computers and technology for analyzing stocks and companies. This real-time data and technology will give your child an introduction to the financial markets and the excitement of stock investing. Some colleges may even offer a virtual trading experience that students can play during their visit. Several times per year we (Linsey and Michelle) partner with North Carolina A&T State University to host TRADER$: Stock Market Experience for its college students and as a field trip for middle school students who visit the campus. This is always a fun and exciting event where we simulate one year of trading in one hour.

Linsey (on the far right) with TRADER$ Stock Market students holding their certificates.

Teach Your Child About Money Through Play

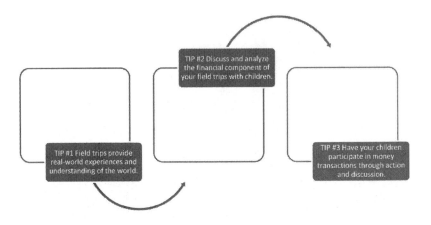

CHAPTER 13

Bonus Chapter: Insurance

This bonus chapter was included because insurance is an important financial literacy topic. Most people have some type of insurance for protection, and it is an expense in their budgets. With insurance in general, the more coverage you add to your plan, the higher the cost. This chapter is an introduction to the four basic types of insurance, with simple activities at the end.

You may feel this is too advanced for younger children; however, many older elementary-aged children and up will be able to understand this concept. It will need to be explained on their level. I encourage you to use the activities at the end of this chapter to deepen their understanding of this topic.

What Is Insurance?

Insurance is a way to prepare yourself in case something bad or misfortunate happens. Examples of misfortunes are chronic illnesses, car accidents, or even someone dying. When these events occur, they can cost a lot of money. If some gets really sick, they may have to get expensive medication or stay in the hospital. Also, it can be very costly to get a car repaired if there is an accident. Furthermore, if a loved one dies, funerals and the cost to bury them can be high. This is why people have insurance.

Insurance moves the risk from individuals or families to insurance companies. The insurance companies collect a huge amount of money from many people to help pay for doctor bills, medication, hospital stays, car repairs, funerals, etc. Insurance can help because not everyone has misfortunes at the same time and the pool of money from everyone covers the costs of those who need it. This is helpful to individuals because the cost of misfortunes can be covered without them paying the full amount.

I will provide you with an example of how insurance works. Let's say you go outside and play with friends on a hot day. You all will most likely get thirsty when you are outside, but you don't know how much water each friend will drink. Instead of everyone bringing their own water and risking one person running out, you all put in a dollar to buy water for everyone. You now have the ability to purchase six cases of water for everyone to drink. Not everyone will need water at the same time, but you will have it ready for those who need it.

Various Types of Insurance

There are various types of insurance, such as health, disability, and auto insurance.

Health Insurance

Your health is what allows you to work, play, socialize, and live in general. If you develop a serious illness or have an accident without being insured, you may not be able to get treatment or may find yourself in a lot of debt to the hospital. This would not be the case for someone who could pay these high costs out of pocket.

Many employers provide health insurance to full-time and some part-time employees. Also, if you are married, both you and your partner may be able to receive health insurance under the same plan. Insurance companies have individual and group plans for business owners as well.

Life Insurance

Life insurance is good to have if you are married and/or have children. Those who are single can have life insurance as well. It helps with many financial needs. If someone in a family dies, the life insurance can help replace the income they made for the family. Sometimes when people die, they leave debt behind, and it must be paid. Life insurance can help pay outstanding debt after a death or pay for the college education of a child left behind. For those who are single, life insurance can pay for costs to bury a family member and debts they leave behind.

Property Insurance

Another term for *property insurance* is *homeowner's insurance*. It is required for most people who own homes. When money is borrowed from a bank to buy a home, they require it to be insured. People who rent can purchase renters' insurance. In case of a burglary, fire, or any disaster, the renters' insurance can cover the replacement costs of your belongings. Furthermore, homeowner and renter's insurance can protect you in case someone injures themselves in your home.

Auto Insurance

Auto or car liability insurance is required in most states in the United States. If you are in a car accident, liability insurance covers damages or repairs to the other car. Another type of insurance is collision, which covers damage to your car. If you buy a car with a loan, you may be required to get collision insurance.

Similar to a house, automobiles can be expensive. If your car gets damaged, you will want to get the car repaired because it transports you to work and school, on errands, etc. Auto insurance can cover injuries or even another driver's death if you are responsible. Furthermore, it can cover legal defense costs as well. If the passengers in your car get hurt during an accident, it can cover their medical treatment as well as yours. Some plans also cover car rentals in case you can't drive your car due to an accident.

ACTIVITIES

The activities below will help your child understand the importance of insurance.

Health Insurance Role Play

- Create a role play with your child where your family goes on a hiking trip and you (the adult) break your arm.
- When your family takes you to the doctor, the bill is $200 for treatment, medication, and a cast.
- You all have insurance, so you only have to pay $40 to the hospital.
- Do the same role play again, but this time you don't have insurance.
    - You may switch roles, where your child gets hurt and you are taking them to the doctor.
- Now you must pay the full $200 for treatment, medication, and a cast.
- Discuss with your child the different outcomes in the scenarios with and without insurance.

Life Insurance Story with Paint

*Please note: If you feel your child is not emotionally ready for this activity, please DON'T DO IT.

- Materials needed
    - Paint
    - Paint brushes
    - Paper
    - Pencil
- Write and paint a story with your child where a family of animals has lost a love one.
    - It could be a family of elephants, fish, lions, etc.
- In the story, the animals would like to plan a nice burial for their lost loved one.
- Brainstorm with your child how they would plan the burial with life insurance financial resources.
- Brainstorm with your child how the burial would be planned with no life insurance.

Property or Homeowners Insurance

Tell your child the scenario below:

- Tony the Tornado has come to your town and ruined everything in your room.

- Luckily, you have paid for homeowners insurance every month.
- The insurance company is going to give you money to replace the items in your room.
- With your child, make a list of what they need replaced in their room.
- Do research on the items and their cost.
- Write a pretend letter to the insurance company requesting the items needed for replacement and their cost.

Auto Insurance

Materials needed:

- Paper
- Art supplies

Directions:

- Have your child draw two cars:
  - Any car that has not been wrecked.
  - The same car but with damage in the back where it has been in a crash.
  - Have your child specify the make, model, and year of the car.

- Tell your child that they hit another car in the back while driving and caused an accident.
- Unfortunately, your child did not have insurance.
- They must pay to get their car fixed as well as the other person's.
- Help your child research how much they will have to pay out of pocket.
- They should research the cost of the car's rear bumper parts such as the following:
  - Reinforcement
  - Absorber
  - Grill
- You may also call an auto body shop and ask them about the typical parts needed when a bumper has been damaged on your child's chosen car.
- Discuss how the scenario would be different if your child had insurance.

MAKE THE WORLD YOUR CHILD'S LEARNING PLAYGROUND

– Andrea Stephenson

Favorite Resources

Rich Dad Poor Dad by Robert Kiyosaki

Rich Kid Smart Kid by Robert Kiyosaki

"100 Children's Books About Money" – https://simplyoutrageousyouth.org/2019/02/07/100-childrens-books-about-money/

CASHFLOW for Kids Game

CASHFLOW 101 Game

The Entrepreneurship Board Game by EE Speaks: https://entrepreneurboardgame.com/products/the-entrepreneur-game-by-eespeaks

Monopoly Board Game

Monopoly Jr. Board Game

Act Your Wage Game by Dave Ramsey

The Game of Life Board Game

Traders Stock Market Experience – Tradersgame.org

Next Steps

Andrea Books *Teach Your Toddler to Read Through Play: Over 130 Games/Activities, Tips, and Resources* and *Fun and Easy Ways to Teach Your Toddler to Write: 135+ Activities, Resources, and Tips for Teaching Writing with Play* are available on Amazon.

Check out our courses, books, and weekly blog posts on our website.

We have more courses and books coming in the future!

Go to our website, SimplyOutrageousYouth.org, and sign in to our SOY Resource Library for accelerated fun learning tips for kids!

THANK YOU!

Thank you so much for investing in this book. For more information or further questions, please contact us at SimplyOutrageousYouth.org.

GOOD DEBT, BAD DEBT ACTIVITY ANSWER KEY

Pick the Good Debt

1. Borrow money for a car wash business

2. Borrow money for a clothing store

3. Borrow money for a gum ball machine

4. Borrow money for a restaurant

5. Borrow money to start a summer camp

Pick Out the Bad Debt

6. Borrow money to buy comic books to collect

7. Borrow money for a video game

8. Borrow money to buy a hair salon

9. Borrow money to buy materials for a lemonade stand

10. Borrow money to buy a shoe store

CALCULATE THE DEBT AND INTEREST ANSWER KEY ACTIVITY

1. (Debt) $24 + (Interest) $9 = $33

2. (Debt) $50 + (Interest) $25 = $75

3. (Debt) $103 + (Interest) $24 = $127

4. (Debt) $111 + (Interest) $30 = $141

5. (Debt) $150 + (Interest) $80 = $230

6. (Debt) $200 + (Interest) $53 = $253

7. (Debt) $533 + (Interest) $64 = $597

8. (Debt) $1,055 + (Interest) $432 = $1,487

9. (Debt) $2,032 + (Interest) $842 = $2,874

10. (Debt) $3,056 + (Interest) $1,477 = $4,533